A-LEVEL YEAR 2

STUDENT GUIDE

EDEXCEL

Economics A

Theme 4

A global perspective

Quintin Brewer

PHILIP ALLAN FOR
HODDER
EDUCATION
AN HACHETTE UK COMPANY

Philip Allan, an imprint of Hodder Education, an Hachette UK company, Blenheim Court, George Street, Banbury, Oxfordshire OX16 5BH

Orders

Bookpoint Ltd, 130 Park Drive, Milton Park, Abingdon, Oxfordshire OX14 4SB

tel: 01235 827827

fax: 01235 400401

e-mail: education@bookpoint.co.uk

Lines are open 9.00 a.m.–5.00 p.m., Monday to Saturday, with a 24-hour message answering service. You can also order through the Hodder Education website: www.hoddereducation.co.uk

© Quintin Brewer 2016

ISBN 978-1-4718-5780-5

First printed 2016

Impression number 5 4

Year 2020 2019 2018 2017

This Guide has been written specifically to support students preparing for the Edexcel A-level Economics examinations. The content has been neither approved nor endorsed by Edexcel and remains the sole responsibility of the author.

Typeset by Integra Software Services Pvt. Ltd., Pondicherry, India

Cover photo: ortodoxfoto/Fotolia

Printed in Dubai

Hachette UK's policy is to use papers that are natural, renewable and recyclable products and made from wood grown in sustainable forests. The logging and manufacturing processes are expected to conform to the environmental regulations of the country of origin.

Contents

Content Guidance

Questions & Answers

Paper 2

Section A

Section B

Section C

Paper 3

■Getting the most from this book

Exam tips

Advice on key points in the text to help you learn and recall content, avoid pitfalls, and polish your exam technique in order to boost your grade.

Knowledge check

Rapid-fire questions throughout the Content Guidance section to check your understanding.

Knowledge check answers

1 Turn to the back of the book for the Knowledge check answers.

Summaries

■ Each core topic is rounded off by a bullet-list summary for quick-check reference of what you need to know.

Exam-style questions

Commentary on the questions

Tips on what you need to do to gain full marks, indicated by the icon ⓔ

Sample student answers

Practise the questions, then look at the student answers that follow.

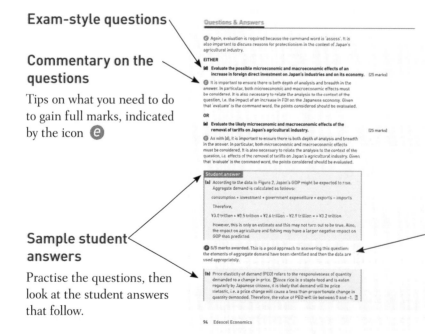

Commentary on sample student answers

Find out how many marks each answer would be awarded in the exam and then read the comments (preceded by the icon ⓔ) following each student answer. Annotations that link back to points made in the student answers show exactly how and where marks are gained or lost.

■ About this book

This guide has been written to prepare students for Theme 4 of Edexcel's Economics A A-level specification (code 9EC0) examinations in economics. It provides an overview of the knowledge and skills required to achieve a high grade in the examination for 'A global perspective'. The specification has been written with very general wording on the concepts to be covered, which allows the examiners more freedom in question setting and the student more opportunity to demonstrate their knowledge and understanding of recent developments. The theme builds on the knowledge and skills gained in Theme 2 'The UK economy — performance and policies'. Theme 4's main emphasis is on globalisation, international trade, poverty and inequality, economic development, the financial sector and the role of the state in the macroeconomy. This theme includes material from Theme 2 — for example, aggregate demand and aggregate supply analysis. More specifically, the following areas are covered:

1 **Globalisation.** As an introduction to this theme we examine the characteristics and causes of globalisation together with an outline of its impacts. Factors limiting globalisation are also examined. This section then explores international payments with particular reference to the balance of payments and exchange rates. Finally, there is an examination of the factors influencing the international competitiveness of a country's goods and services.

2 **Poverty and inequality.** In this section we consider the causes, consequences and measurement of poverty and inequality.

3 **Emerging and developing countries.** The factors influencing growth and development are examined, followed by an analysis of strategies which influence growth and development.

4 **The financial sector.** Given the significance of money and finance in the financial crisis, this area has been restored as an important area of study in A-level economics. The role of financial markets, market failure in this sector and the role of central banks in the economy are considered.

5 **The role of the state in the macroeconomy.** In this section, all aspects of public finance (public expenditure, taxation, fiscal deficits and national debts) are considered. Building on concepts covered in Theme 2, this is followed by an examination of the use of macroeconomic policies (demand-side, supply-side and direct controls) in a global context. The problems facing policymakers in applying these policies are also examined.

This guide is aimed at developing your macroeconomics skills in a global context, and should be used alongside your notes and other revision aids in the second year of study of Advanced Economics. The guide includes typical questions and answers, and explains what the examiners are looking for. Common mistakes are highlighted and several strategies for increasing your marks are suggested.

- The **Content Guidance** section provides an overview of the main topics, identifying what has to be learned and explaining the theoretical requirements of the theme.

- The **Questions & Answers** section provides questions and answers on the economic concepts and topics in Theme 4, together with explanation of the exam format and the skills that will be tested. Examiner's comments on the questions are indicated by the icon **ⓔ**. A selection of student answers is provided to give you an idea of the level of answer required to achieve a grade A. These answers are interspersed with examiner's comments (indicated by the icon **ⓔ**) to help you to get to know the expectations of those who will mark your papers. After reviewing the Theme 4 topics, you should try these sample questions, ideally under timed conditions, and then compare your work with the answers and comments provided. This will allow you to identify areas of weakness that require further work.

Content Guidance

■ International economics

Globalisation

The meaning of globalisation

There is no precise definition of the term 'globalisation'. It is used to refer to a variety of ways in which countries are becoming more and more closely integrated, not just in the economic sense, but also culturally and politically.

However, one of the best definitions of globalisation in the economic sense is by Peter Jay, who was the BBC's economics correspondent in 1996: 'The ability to produce any good or service anywhere in the world, using raw materials, components, capital and technology from anywhere, sell the resulting output anywhere and place the profits anywhere.'

Globalisation is not a new phenomenon because there have been many periods in history when there was considerable integration between countries; for example, during the height of the Roman Empire. However, the pace of global integration has increased considerably over the last 50 years.

Characteristics of globalisation

Globalisation, in the economic sense, is characterised by the following:

■ An increase in trade as a proportion of world GDP. Figure 1 shows how trade has been growing at a faster rate than gross domestic product (GDP).

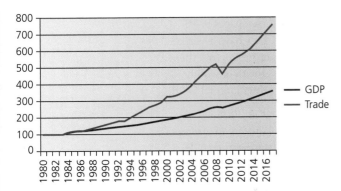

Figure 1 World GDP and global trade (1980 = 100)
Source: www.worldbank.org

■ Increased movements of financial capital and people between countries.

Exam tip

Globalisation is a central concept in this section so it is important that you fully understand its key features.

Content Guidance

- Increased international specialisation and division of labour. It is increasingly common for parts and components of products to be made in different countries and for assembly to occur in another country.
- The growing importance of global or transnational companies (TNCs).
- An increase in **foreign direct investment (FDI)**.

Factors contributing to globalisation

A variety of factors have contributed to the increased economic integration of countries.

- One of the most significant is the *fall in transport costs*. In real terms the price of transporting goods has decreased significantly, enabling goods to be imported and exported more cheaply.
- Coupled with this has been a *decline in the cost of communications*. In particular, the cost of using the internet has fallen greatly over the last 20 years and its availability has increased.
- The *lowering of trade barriers* since the Second World War has been a major factor in the growth of world trade. The World Trade Organization (WTO) — formerly the General Agreement on Tariffs and Trade — has been responsible for negotiating reductions in tariffs and other barriers to trade in rounds of talks, the most recent of which is the Doha Round.
- Both the *collapse of communism* and the *opening up of China* to world trade have contributed to globalisation. Countries which were previously not open to FDI became much more integrated into the world trading system.
- *Transnational (global) companies* have taken advantage of the reduction in trade barriers and the development of the internet to organise trade on a global scale.
- *Growth in the number and size of trading blocs* (*regional trade agreements*) has resulted in increased trade between the member countries of these blocs. These are considered in more detail on pages 13–14.

Impacts of globalisation

On countries

Free trade enables the application of the *law of comparative advantage* (see pages 9–10), which suggests that, when countries specialise in the goods in which they have a comparative advantage (i.e. the goods can be produced at a lower opportunity cost), then world output and living standards will increase. It is evident that the growth of world trade in both goods and services has been associated with increased growth in real GDP.

However, the global financial crisis that became particularly evident in 2008 led to a period of *deglobalisation*, in which countries adopt protectionist policies in an attempt to protect domestic employment. This leads to a decline in specialisation and trade. More recently, trade has recovered.

Further, globalisation has also been associated with *increased inequality* within developed countries. As much manufacturing has been transferred to developing countries, the demand for unskilled workers has declined in developed countries, resulting in a fall in their wages relative to those of skilled workers.

Foreign direct investment (FDI) Cross-border investment by a business in one economy with the objective of obtaining a lasting interest in an enterprise resident in another economy. It may involve the acquisition by a business in one country of a business in another country.

Knowledge check 1

How might a significant increase in transport costs affect globalisation?

8 Edexcel Economics A

On governments

If globalisation results in an increase in economic growth and, therefore, in incomes, then governments should receive extra tax revenues. However, **transfer pricing** by global companies may result in lower tax revenue from corporation tax.

On producers and consumers

- For producers, there are likely to be benefits in terms of lower production costs as a result of offshoring and also economies of scale.
- For consumers, globalisation may mean a wider choice of goods. Further, prices may be lower, leading to an increase in consumer surplus.

On workers

Globalisation has been criticised on the basis that it has *promoted exploitation* of workers, including the use of child labour. It is argued that globalisation has driven down wages (especially those of unskilled workers) as a share of GDP. Further, health and safety laws and regulations are usually less demanding in developing countries, which might have detrimental effects on the workforce.

On the environment

The *external costs* associated with increasing globalisation are becoming increasingly apparent, especially in relation to increased trade, air travel and environmental degradation. Global warming associated with various forms of pollution arising from increased trade is one example of external costs arising from increased globalisation.

> **Exam tip**
>
> The effects of globalisation overlap with many other areas of this section, so it is useful to revisit these once you have understood those topics.

Specialisation and trade

Absolute and comparative advantage

This law states that, even if one country has an **absolute advantage** in the production of all goods, it can still benefit from specialisation and trade if it specialises in the production of goods in which it has a **comparative advantage** (i.e. if it specialises in the production of those products in which its opportunity cost is lowest). The crucial requirement is that there must be a difference in the opportunity cost of producing the products.

Assumptions underlying the theory of comparative advantage

- No transport costs.
- No trade barriers.
- Constant returns to scale, i.e. average cost of production is constant.
- Perfect mobility of resources between different uses.
- Buyers/consumers have perfect knowledge.

Transfer pricing When a global company manages its accounting of internal transactions within the company to show the highest profits in the country in which corporation tax is lowest.

Knowledge check 2

What is the link between savings ratios and global imbalances?

Absolute advantage When a country can produce more of a product than another country.

Comparative advantage When a country can produce a product at a lower opportunity cost than another country, so it has a relative advantage in producing that product.

The following example illustrates the theory of comparative advantage.

Suppose countries A and B both produce two products — palm oil and televisions. They can both produce the following amounts of these products with the same quantity of resources:

Country	Palm oil	Televisions
A	20,000	10,000
B	8,000	8,000

Clearly, country A has an absolute advantage in the production of both palm oil and televisions. If each country devotes half its resources to the production of each product, then output will be as follows:

Country	Palm oil	Televisions
A	10,000	5,000
B	4,000	4,000
Total	14,000	9,000

To determine whether trade will be worthwhile, the *opportunity costs* must be calculated:

	Opportunity cost of producing 1 kilogram of palm oil	Opportunity cost of producing 1 television
A	½	2
B	1	1

From the table, it can be seen that country A has a comparative advantage in palm oil (because the opportunity cost is lower), while country B has a comparative advantage in televisions.

For trade to be beneficial, the terms of trade must lie between the opportunity cost ratios. In this case, the terms of trade must lie between 1 kilogram of palm oil and 2 kilograms of palm oil for one television.

The terms of trade are measured as follows:

$$\frac{\text{index of export prices}}{\text{index of import prices}} \times 100$$

You should note that, if the opportunity costs were the same, then there would be no benefit from specialisation and trade.

Limitations of the principle of comparative advantage

- Transport costs might outweigh the benefits of comparative advantage.
- Similarly, trade barriers might distort comparative advantage.
- Increased specialisation and production might result in rising average costs caused by diseconomies of scale.

However, despite these limitations, many economists support the view that free trade brings net benefits to the global economy.

Exam tip

It is useful to learn a numerical example to illustrate comparative advantage for use in an examination.

Advantages and disadvantages of specialisation and trade

Advantages

- Efficient resource allocation: specialisation and free trade based on comparative advantage result in an efficient allocation of resources.
- Higher world output and, therefore, higher living standards.
- Lower prices and more choice for consumers.
- Incentive for domestic producers to become more efficient.
- Larger markets for firms, enabling them to benefit from economies of scale.

Disadvantages

- The law of comparative advantage is based on unrealistic assumptions (see above).
- For developing economies, specialisation in the production of primary products might prevent diversification into more productive manufacturing industries.
- There is a danger of overdependence on imports, especially those of strategic importance.
- A country's goods and services may be uncompetitive, resulting in a persistent trade deficit.

Knowledge check 3

What are the main benefits of free trade?

Patterns of trade

Factors influencing the pattern of trade

The pattern of world trade changes over time, as shown in Figure 2. It may be explained by a range of factors, including the following:

- *Changes in comparative advantage*. Comparative advantage may change as a result of factors such as changes in labour skills and productivity, discovery of new natural resources and the adoption of new technology.
- *Emerging economies*. The pattern of world trade has also been greatly affected by the growth of emerging economies, for example China, which is now a major manufacturer.

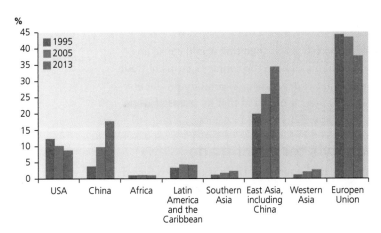

Figure 2 Change in regional share in global manufacturing exports, 1995–2013
Source: UNCTADStat.

■ *Trading blocs and bilateral trading agreements*. Since the Second World War there has been a significant growth in the number and size of **trading blocs**. Given that most of these have free trade between member countries and that customs unions have common external tariffs, trading blocs have had an important influence on the pattern of world trade. Similarly, bilateral trade agreements (agreements between two countries) have also affected trade patterns.

■ *Changes in relative exchange rates*. A long-term change in a country's exchange rate against those of other countries will affect the relative competitiveness of that country's goods and services and so will influence trading patterns. For example, if country A's currency depreciates against those of other countries, then its goods and services will become more competitive and so its exports are likely to increase and imports decrease relative to those of other countries.

> **Trading bloc** A group of countries that trade freely but protect themselves from imports from non-members.

Terms of trade

Calculation of the terms of trade

The **terms of trade** (T/T) are calculated by using the following formula:

$$\text{T/T} = \frac{\text{index of export prices}}{\text{index of import prices}} \times 100$$

Therefore, the terms of trade is the relationship between the price of exports and the price of imports or the rate at which exports exchange for imports.

> **Terms of trade** The average price of a country's exports relative to the average price of its imports.

Factors influencing a country's terms of trade

The following are examples of some of the factors which can influence a country's terms of trade.

■ *Relative inflation rates*. If the UK inflation rate is higher than that of its trading partners then export prices will be rising relative to import prices, so causing a rise in the UK's terms of trade.

■ *Changes in raw material prices*. For a developed country which imports most of its raw materials, a rise in imported raw material prices would cause a fall in its terms of trade.

■ *Changes in exchange rates*. If a country's exchange rate increases relative to those of other countries then its export prices would rise and its import prices would fall, so causing its terms of trade to increase.

■ *Tariffs*. If a country imposes a tariff on imported goods then this would cause an increase in import prices and so would result in a fall in the country's terms of trade.

■ *Dependency on primary products*. If a country is dependent on primary products then according to the *Prebisch–Singer hypothesis* it may find that its terms of trade decrease over time (see page 35).

Impact of changes in a country's terms of trade

■ *On living standards*. An upward movement in the terms of trade is usually referred to as an 'improvement' because it implies that the country has to export less to buy a given quantity of imports. This implies a higher standard of living for the citizens of that country. In contrast, a fall in the terms of trade is referred to as a 'deterioration' because it implies that more must be exported to gain a given quantity of imports, which, in turn, implies a fall in living standards.

- *On the balance of payments on current account.* An upward movement in a country's terms of trade would decrease the competitiveness of its goods and services because its export prices would be rising relative to its import prices. Consequently, the country's balance of payments on current account is likely to deteriorate. In turn, this could cause a depreciation in its exchange rate (see page 20).
- *On the rate of inflation.* A fall in a country's terms of trade may be associated with a higher rate of inflation if the fall was caused by an increase in the price of imported raw materials.
- *On developing countries.* Resource-rich developing countries sometimes suffer from what is called the 'resource curse'. This arises because ownership of minerals and fuels causes an appreciation in the exchange rates of the currencies of these countries and, in turn, an increase in the terms of trade. This results in a loss of competitiveness of their manufactured goods and services, leading to slower economic growth than might otherwise have been the case.

Knowledge check 4

What factors could cause an increase in a country's terms of trade?

Trading blocs and the World Trade Organization (WTO)

Types of trading bloc

Regional trade blocs are intergovernmental associations that manage and promote trade activities for specific regions of the world. Trading blocs may take several forms:

- *Free trade areas.* Trade barriers are removed between member countries, but individual members can still impose tariffs and quotas on countries outside the area. An example is the North Atlantic Free Trade Area (NAFTA).
- *Customs unions.* The characteristics of customs unions include free trade between member states and a *common external tariff* on goods imported from outside the bloc. Examples include the European Union (EU) and the Customs Union of Russia, Belarus and Kazakhstan (formed in 2010).
- *Common markets.* These are customs unions but with the added dimension that it is not only goods and services that can be moved freely within the area (between member states), but also factors of production (especially labour). Examples include Mercosur and the East African Common Market.
- *Monetary unions.* These are customs unions that adopt a *common currency.* The eurozone area of the EU is an example of such a union.

Exam tip

Trading blocs are not blocks on trade such as tariffs; they are groups of countries that agree to trade freely between themselves.

Costs and benefits of regional trade agreements

Costs

- *Trade diversion.* Trade may be diverted away from low-cost producers outside the bloc to high-cost producers within the bloc because of the existence of tariffs on goods from outside the bloc.
- *Distortion of comparative advantage.* The existence of trade restrictions on goods from countries outside the agreement will distort comparative advantage and lead to a less efficient allocation of resources, lowering global economic growth.
- *Loss of independent monetary policy.* This would be relevant to countries in monetary unions which would be unable to control their own interest rates and exchange rates.

Benefits
- *Trade creation*. The removal of trade barriers between member countries of the bloc will result in increased specialisation and trade between them.
- *Increase in FDI*. Global companies may wish to invest inside a trading bloc to avoid trade restrictions.

In addition, monetary unions may enjoy further benefits, including the following:
- *Elimination of transactions costs*. In other words, there would be no costs involved in changing currencies when goods are imported or exported.
- *Price transparency*. A single currency means that consumers have the ability to compare prices more easily across national borders.
- *Elimination of currency fluctuations between member countries*. This eliminates uncertainty and might help to attract FDI.

Role of the WTO in trade liberalisation

Essentially, the WTO performs two key functions:
- to promote free trade among the 188 member countries through so-called 'rounds of talks'
- to settle trade disputes between members

Possible conflicts between regional trade agreements and the WTO

The existence of trading blocs has two significant consequences, as described above:
- trade creation
- trade diversion

While trade creation is a goal of the WTO, the trade diversion which results from regional trade agreements clearly is not.

Nevertheless, it may be argued that the growth in both the number and size of regional trade agreements has contributed to the WTO goal of promoting free trade.

Restrictions on free trade

Reasons for restrictions on free trade

The term 'protectionism' refers to measures designed to limit free trade. Arguments supporting the need for protectionism include the following:
- *To protect infant industries*. This argument might be particularly relevant to developing countries that are in the process of industrialisation. Without protection, infant industries might be unable to compete because they have yet to establish themselves and are too small to benefit from economies of scale.
- *To protect geriatric industries*. These are industries that might demand protection so that they have time to restructure and rationalise production, which would enable them to become competitive once again. Typically, these occur in developed economies that are losing their comparative advantage.

> **Knowledge check 5**
>
> What is the key feature of any regional trade agreement (trading bloc)?

- *To ensure employment protection.* Cheap imports might threaten jobs in the domestic economy and workers might demand that the government takes action to limit imports.
- *To prevent dumping.* 'Dumping' refers to goods being exported to another country at below the average cost of production. It is a form of **predatory pricing** and, if it can be proved, is illegal under the WTO rules. This is one of the few arguments in favour of protectionism that can be justified in terms of economic theory because it unfairly distorts comparative advantage.
- *To correct a balance of payments deficit on current account.* Restrictions on imports might help to reduce the imbalance between the value of imports and the value of exports. However, under a system of floating exchange rates, it is possible that this correction will happen automatically.
- *To restrict imports from countries whose health and safety regulations and environmental regulations are less stringent.* Some argue that developing countries might have an unfair competitive advantage because production is not subject to the same laws and regulations that apply to developed countries, so enabling them to produce at a lower average cost.
- *For strategic reasons.* A country might introduce protectionist policies on goods of strategic importance in time of war so that it is not dependent on imports. Food, defence equipment and energy are items frequently used as examples of such goods.
- *To raise tax revenue.* Tariffs might be an important source of tax revenue for developing countries.
- *In retaliation.* Barriers to trade might be imposed by a country because another country has restricted the import of its goods.

Types of restrictions on trade

There are numerous ways by which free trade can be prevented. The most common are *tariffs, quotas, subsidies to domestic producers* and *non-tariff barriers*. In countries where the exchange rate is not freely floating, the authorities might also hold down the value of the currency artificially to give their goods a competitive advantage.

Tariffs

These are sometimes referred to as customs duties: they are simply taxes on imported goods. Figure 3 illustrates the effect of a tariff.

> **Predatory pricing**
> A deliberate strategy by a firm aimed at driving competitors out of the market by setting its prices below average variable costs.

> **Exam tip**
> Knowledge of the tariff diagram is very useful in explaining a range of possible effects.

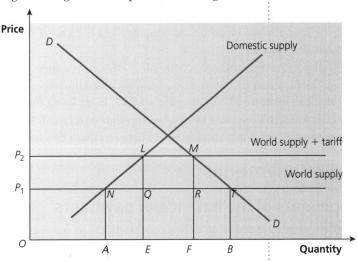

Figure 3 The effects of imposing a tariff

Before the tariff is imposed:

- the price paid by consumers is OP_1
- domestic output is OA
- imports are AB

Once the tariff is imposed:

- the price paid by consumers rises to P_2, so reducing consumer surplus by P_1P_2MT
- domestic output rises to OE, so increasing producer surplus by P_1P_2LN
- imports fall to EF
- tax revenue to the government is $QLMR$
- net welfare loss areas are NLQ and RMT

Quotas

Import quotas place a physical restriction on the amount of goods that can be imported. They have similar effects to those of tariffs, in that the price of imported goods will rise and domestic producers should gain more business. However, unlike tariffs, the government does not receive any revenue.

Subsidies to domestic producers

Grants given to domestic producers by the government artificially lower their production costs, so enabling their goods to be more competitive. Subsidies therefore act as a barrier to trade.

Non-tariff barriers

These take a variety of forms, including labelling, health and safety regulations, environmental standards and documentation in country of origin. In effect, such regulations increase the costs of foreign producers and so act as a barrier to trade.

Impact of protectionist policies

- *On consumers.* Higher prices and less choice.
- *On producers.* Less incentive for domestic producers to become more efficient.
- *On governments.* A government would receive tax revenue from tariffs but subsidies to domestic producers would incur a cost on taxpayers. Once such barriers are introduced, it might prove to be difficult to remove them because of the adverse effect on domestic producers.
- *On living standards.* Protectionism results in a less efficient resource allocation because trade barriers distort comparative advantage and reduce specialisation, which will result in lower world output and, therefore, lower living standards.
- *On equality.* Trade barriers imposed by developed countries on goods from developing economies could increase inequality between these two sets of countries.

Balance of payments

The components of the balance of payments

The balance of payments is a record of all financial transactions between one country and other countries. When there is an inflow of foreign currency into the UK, this is recorded as a positive item, whereas when there is an outflow of foreign currency, this is recorded as a negative item.

The main components of the balance of payments are the *current account* and the *capital and financial account* (formerly called the capital account).

The current account

This is composed of the following:

- *The trade balance*. This is the value of goods and services exported minus the value of goods and services imported. The trade balance may be separated into the *trade in goods balance* and the *trade in services balance*.
- *The income balance (now renamed primary income)*. This is income flows into the country from non-residents minus income flows out of the country from residents to non-residents. Income refers to compensation to employees and investment income, for example.
- *Current transfers (now renamed secondary income)*. This relates to items such as food aid and the UK's contribution to the EU's Common Agricultural Policy (CAP).

The capital and financial account

This comprises transactions associated with changes of ownership of the UK's foreign financial assets and liabilities. A key factor influencing the financial account is foreign direct investment (FDI). Also included are portfolio investment in shares and bonds, changes in foreign exchange reserves and the short-term capital flows, often referred to as 'hot money' flows, associated with speculation.

The balance on this account should exactly offset the current account balance (although, in practice, there is a significant component comprising errors and omissions).

Causes of deficits and surpluses on the current account

Causes of current account deficits

These include:

- relatively low productivity, meaning that the country's goods and services are not competitive internationally
- relatively high inflation rate
- overvalued exchange rate
- dependence on highly priced imported raw materials
- relocation of manufacturing industries to low-wage countries
- protectionism by other countries

Causes of current account surpluses

These include:

- relatively high productivity, meaning that the country's goods and services are more internationally competitive
- relatively low inflation rate
- undervalued exchange rate
- abundance of minerals, fuels and agricultural produce which is in high demand by other countries

- relocation of manufacturing industries from high-wage countries
- protectionist policies designed to reduce imports

The UK's current account

For many years, the UK has had a deficit on the current account. In particular, the trade in goods balance has deteriorated over a number of years, as shown in Figure 4.

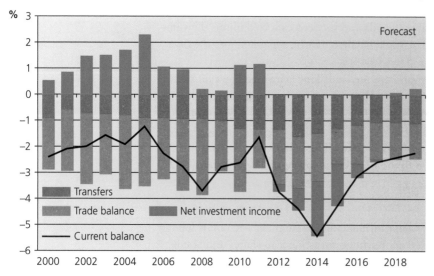

Figure 4 The UK balance of payments on current account
Source: www.ons.gov.uk

The main reasons for the UK's current account deficit include:

- the high value of sterling 1996–2008
- continuous economic growth 1992–2008 — the UK has a high marginal propensity to import and so rising real incomes have led to a significant increase in imports
- relatively low productivity of the UK's workers, resulting in higher average costs
- the relocation of manufacturing to countries with lower labour costs (e.g. China and eastern European countries)
- the eurozone crisis since 2009, which has meant slow growth and weak demand for the UK's exports
- the deterioration in 'net income balance', i.e. net income from interest, profits and dividends
- the 'Chindia effect' — the industrialisation of China and India has led to a flood of cheap imports into the UK

Measures to reduce a country's imbalance on the current account

Possible measures to reduce a *current account deficit* include the following:

- *Supply-side policies designed to increase productivity and competition.* These would help to improve the competitiveness of the country's goods and services and so lead to an increase in exports and a decrease in imports. Examples of supply-side polices include:
  - education and training aimed at increasing the productivity of the workforce

Knowledge check 7

What factors might cause a balance of trade surplus?

- tax breaks and investment allowances to stimulate purchase of capital equipment
- measures to promote small- and medium-sized businesses to promote competition
- privatisation, deregulation and contracting out of public services

■ *Expenditure-reducing policies*. These could include deflationary fiscal policy, i.e. measures to reduce aggregate demand by raising taxes and/or decreasing government expenditure. If direct taxes were raised then disposable income would fall, causing a fall in consumption and, consequently, a fall in imports, so resulting in an improvement in the balance of trade.

NB Many countries have independent central banks so it is not within their power to raise interest rates as a means of reducing a current account deficit.

■ *Expenditure-switching policies*. These include:

- *protectionist policies* such as tariffs, quotas and subsidies to domestic producers. However, it should be noted that WTO rules and membership of trading blocs might make it impossible/illegal to employ these measures.
- *devaluation/depreciation of the country's currency*. A country with a fixed exchange rate could devalue its currency. However, under a system of floating exchange rates, a depreciation of the exchange rate of the country's currency could only be engineered by reducing interest rates or through quantitative easing, but these monetary tools would not be available to a government if the central bank were independent. A detailed analysis of the effects of a depreciation/devaluation of the exchange rate of a country's currency is considered on pages 22–24.

> **Knowledge check 8**
>
> What is the distinction between expenditure-switching and expenditure-reducing policies?

Significance of global trade imbalances

Like the UK, the USA has experienced large current account deficits, while, in contrast, China has experienced huge current account surpluses. Whether such global imbalances can be sustained in the long run is a major question.

On the one hand, if the deficits are easily financed by inflows on the financial account, there may be no cause for concern. Further, under a system of floating exchange rates, over time, there should be an automatic adjustment (i.e. a deficit would cause the exchange rate to fall). On the other hand, continuous deficits by the USA have, in effect, been financed by the Chinese, which may not be a sustainable option in the long run.

Exchange rates

The *nominal exchange rate* is the number of units of the domestic currency that can purchase a unit of a given foreign currency.

The *real exchange rate* is calculated to measure the movements of the competitiveness of the country's currency vis-à-vis another country's currency on the basis of the inflation differential between the countries. In other words, the real exchange rate is the nominal exchange rate adjusted to reflect the different inflation rates in the countries of the two currencies concerned.

Effective exchange rates are estimated to measure the movements of a country's currency value or average exchange rate in a basket of currencies of trading partner countries.

A country's *trade-weighted exchange rate* is a common form of the effective exchange rate. It is the average exchange rate of a basket of currencies, weighted by the amount of trade with each country.

Exchange rate systems

The exchange rate is the rate at which one currency exchanges for another. In other words it is the *price* of one currency in terms of another, e.g. £1 = $1.50. There are three main exchange rate systems: floating, fixed and managed.

Floating exchange rates

Under a system of floating exchange rates, market forces (supply of, and demand for, the currency in the foreign exchange market) determine the value at which one currency exchanges for another.

Fixed exchange rates

Under a system of fixed exchange rates, the value at which one currency exchanges for another is fixed by the central bank or the government against another currency or a basket of currencies or gold.

Managed exchange rates

Under a system of managed exchange rates, market forces determine the value at which one currency exchanges for another but intervention by the central bank influences the exchange rate of the currency.

Distinction between revaluation and appreciation

A *revaluation* of a currency only occurs under a system of fixed exchange rates when the government decides to increase the value of its currency against other currencies or gold. *Appreciation* of a currency occurs under a system of floating exchange rates when the value of a currency increases against another currency as a result of the operation of market forces.

Distinction between devaluation and depreciation

A *devaluation* of a currency only occurs under a system of fixed exchange rates when the government decides to decrease the value of its currency against other currencies or gold. *Depreciation* of a currency occurs under a system of floating exchange rates when the value of a currency decreases against another currency as a result of the operation of market forces.

Factors influencing the value of a currency					
Relative inflation rates	Relative interest rates	The state of the economy	The balance of payments on current account	Political factors	Speculation

Figure 5 Factors influencing the exchange rate of a country's currency

As Figure 5 shows, a variety of factors can influence the value of a country's currency against other currencies, including the following:

- *Relative inflation rates.* If the country's inflation rate is higher than that of its major competitors then, according to *purchasing power parity (PPP) analysis*, it would be expected that the value of the currency would fall. The PPP rate is the rate at which a particular product would be sold at the same price in the UK and abroad when expressed in a common currency.
- *Relative interest rates.* If the UK has higher interest rates than those of other countries, then foreigners with surplus balances are likely to place them in UK banks, so increasing the demand for sterling and causing the value of the pound to increase.
- *The state of the economy.* If, for example, the UK economy is performing well, this will increase the confidence of speculators and foreign investors, who will buy sterling, so causing its value to rise.
- *The balance of payments on current account.* If there is a persistent deficit on the current account, then the supply of the currency would be high relative to demand for it and the value of the currency would be expected to fall. In practice, this factor is not significant because the flows of money associated with trade are small compared with 'hot money' flows and other transactions recorded in the financial account.
- *Political stability.* In developing countries, instability may cause a loss of confidence in the country's currency.
- *Speculation.* The exchange rate might be affected by speculation concerning a range of possible events, including factors such as the future state of the economy, a change in government or impending strikes. For example, if it is expected that the economy will recover from a recession much more quickly than originally thought, then speculators may buy sterling, so pushing up its value.

Government intervention in currency markets

There are two main ways by which the exchange rate of a currency against other currencies may be influenced: foreign currency transactions and interest rates.

Foreign currency transactions

The central bank can intervene in the foreign exchange market in attempts to influence the exchange rate of its currency against other currencies.

To bring about an appreciation in the exchange rate of the currency against other currencies, the central bank would buy its currency on the foreign exchange market in exchange for foreign currency. The increase in demand for the domestic currency would cause an increase in its value against foreign currencies.

In contrast, to engineer a depreciation of the exchange rate of its currency, the central bank would sell its own country's currency on the foreign exchange market in exchange for foreign currency. This increase in supply would cause a fall in the value of the currency against foreign currencies.

Knowledge check 9

What is likely to happen to the value of the euro if members of the eurozone default on their debts?

Use of interest rates

To bring about an appreciation of the currency against other currencies, the central bank would raise interest rates. For example, in December 2014, the Central Bank of Russia raised interest rates to 17% with the aim of making it more attractive for foreign citizens to place money in Russia's banks, so increasing demand for roubles on the foreign exchange market.

A reduction in interest rates would have the opposite effect, making it less attractive for citizens and foreign nationals to hold money in that country's banks. This would cause an increase in supply of the currency on the foreign exchange market and so reduce its value against other currencies.

Competitive devaluation/depreciation

The meaning of competitive devaluations/depreciations

Competitive devaluations or depreciations are sometimes referred to as **currency wars** because a devaluation/depreciation by one country results in other countries taking measures to devalue their currencies.

Currency war When a country deliberately reduces the value of its currency in order to gain a competitive advantage and this results in other countries taking similar action.

The effects of competitive devaluations/depreciations

These could cause:

- an increase in the rate of inflation because imports would become more expensive
- a decline in world trade because of the uncertainties associated with fluctuating exchange rates

Further, countries could retaliate by imposing protectionist measures, e.g. tariffs, as happened in the 1930s.

Effects of a change in the exchange rate of a currency

On the current account of the balance of payments

A depreciation/devaluation makes a country's goods and services more competitive and so should lead to an improvement in its current account.

Suppose that the value of the pound against the dollar falls, e.g. from £1 = $2.00 to £1 = $1.50. There are two effects.

- It will make the price of goods exported from the UK *decrease* in the country of sale (e.g. a bottle of UK whisky costing £20 would have sold for $40 in the USA but will now sell for $30).
- It will make the price of goods imported into the UK *increase* (e.g. a $10 bottle of Californian wine would have been priced at £5 in the UK but will now cost £6.67).

Therefore, a fall in the value of the pound makes UK goods more competitive.

The consequence of this is that demand for exports is likely to rise while demand for imports is likely to fall. This is likely to cause a reduction in the size of the deficit on the current account of the balance of payments.

Exam tip

Remember that a fall in the value of a country's currency causes an increase in the price competitiveness of its goods and services, whereas a rise causes a decrease in the price competitiveness of that country's goods and services.

The Marshall–Lerner condition

For there to be an improvement in the current account, the Marshall–Lerner condition must be fulfilled — i.e. the sum of the price elasticities of demand (PEDs) for imports and exports must be greater than 1.

The J-curve effect

It is possible that there could be a time lag before the full effects of the depreciation of the currency work through the economy, such that the sum of the price elasticities of demand would be less than 1 in the short run but greater than 1 in the long run. This gives rise to the *J-curve effect*, as illustrated in Figure 6.

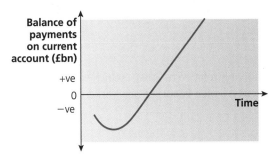

Figure 6 The J-curve effect

Initially, the current account deteriorates, since demand for imports is price inelastic because of contracts or stocks of goods. Also, demand for exports may be inelastic because it takes time for consumers to adjust to the price changes. In the longer term, demand for both imports and exports may become more elastic and, if the Marshall–Lerner condition is fulfilled, the current account will improve.

On economic growth and employment/unemployment

If there is an increase in net exports following a depreciation in the value of a country's currency against other currencies, then aggregate demand (AD) will increase, causing an increase in real output. In turn this should result in an increase in employment and a decrease in unemployment.

On the rate of inflation

Following a depreciation, inflationary pressures could arise from two sources:

- The increase in AD, described above, resulting from a rise in net exports.
- Imported inflation: the rise in import prices, especially of raw materials and commodities, is likely to increase costs of production, causing a leftward shift in the aggregate supply curve and therefore an increase in the rate of inflation

On foreign direct investment (FDI) flows

A depreciation in the exchange rate of country A's currency against others would potentially make it more attractive for foreign companies to invest in that country because a unit of a foreign currency would buy more units of country A's currency.

However, if the depreciation is indicative of a lack of confidence in the country's economy, then FDI inflows may not increase.

Knowledge check 10

What would be the effect on the current account of the balance of payments following a depreciation in the value of the currency if the sum of PEDs for exports and imports were between 0 and –1?

International competitiveness

A country's 'international competitiveness' refers to its ability to sell its goods and services in domestic and international markets at a price and quality that is attractive in those markets. Competitiveness may be measured in terms of *price* or *non-price factors*. The non-price factors include quality, design, reliability and availability.

Measures of international competitiveness

Relative unit labour costs

This refers to the measurement of labour costs in one country relative to those in another country. To make international comparisons, the figures are converted into a single currency and expressed as an index number.

Relative export prices

These might be affected by factors such as productivity (relative to other countries). This may be measured in terms of labour productivity, which is output per worker per hour worked.

The global competiveness index

This is a composite measure devised by the World Economic Forum and is based on factors such as infrastructure, macroeconomic stability, health and education, degree of efficiency in the labour and goods market, technological readiness and innovation.

The top 10 rankings for 2014–15 were:

1 Swizerland
2 Singapore
3 USA
4 Finland
5 Germany
6 Japan
7 Hong Kong SAR
8 Netherlands
9 UK
10 Sweden

Factors influencing international competitiveness

Real exchange rate

Competitiveness is determined by a variety of factors but one of the most important is a country's **real exchange rate**, which is the nominal exchange rate adjusted for changes in price levels between economies.

More precisely:

$$\text{real exchange rate} = \frac{\text{nominal exchange rate} \times \text{domestic price level}}{\text{foreign price level}}$$

There will be a depreciation in the real exchange rate if the nominal exchange rate falls or if the prices of goods abroad rise relative to prices in the home country. Therefore, a fall in the real exchange rate will cause an increase in the competitiveness of a country's goods.

Real exchange rate
The nominal exchange rate adjusted to reflect the different inflation rates (and, therefore, purchasing power) of the currencies concerned.

In contrast, the real exchange rate will increase if the nominal exchange rate rises or if the UK price level rises relative to the foreign price level. Consequently, an appreciation of the real exchange rate is associated with a fall in the country's competitiveness.

Wage costs and non-wage costs

Wage costs are the most important cost of production for many industries. Consequently, if wages are higher in the UK than in China, it is likely that the prices of goods in the UK will be higher than those of China. However, the relationship between labour productivity and wages is crucial in influencing unit labour costs.

Non-wage costs are also significant for international competitiveness. These include:

- national insurance contributions paid by employers (taxes on employment)
- health and safety regulations
- environmental regulations
- employment protection and anti-discrimination laws
- contributions into company pension schemes

These non-wage costs are frequently much higher in developed countries than in developing countries and so have the effect of reducing the international competitiveness of goods and services from developed countries.

Other factors

Governments can try to improve international competitiveness through a variety of *supply-side policies*. Of particular relevance are the following:

- *Education and training schemes* which may increase the occupational mobility of labour. Education and training influence the level of *human capital*, which is defined as the knowledge and skills of the workforce.
- *Public sector reform* aimed at reducing red tape and regulations.
- Government expenditure to improve *infrastructure* (e.g. roads, railways, telecommunications, power generating stations and water supply).
- *Privatisation and deregulation*.
- Incentives for *investment* such as tax breaks if companies use profits for investment or for research and redevelopment.
- Measures to increase *labour market flexibility* such as making it easier to hire and fire workers, reducing the strength of trade unions and allowing the use of flexible hours contracts.

It should be noted that international agreements are likely to prevent individual countries increasing their competitiveness by raising tariffs. For example, the UK cannot simply introduce tariffs on goods from other EU countries because of its legal obligations as a member of the EU. Similarly, most countries are members of the WTO, whose rules prevent a country unilaterally imposing protectionist measures unless there is justifiable case.

Further, it is not possible for the UK government to devalue its currency because the pound is a floating currency. Also, since the Bank of England is independent, the government cannot directly engineer a depreciation in the exchange rate of the pound through a reduction in interest rates because control over interest rates is no longer in its hands.

Exam tip

Remember to include both price and non-price factors in discussions of international competitiveness.

Exam tip

Refer back to what you learned in Theme 2 about supply-side policies and look out for new measures being introduced by governments.

The significance of international competitiveness

Benefits of being internationally competitive

A country can enjoy several advantages of being internationally competitive, including:

- a surplus on its current account of the balance of payments
- export-led growth
- low levels of unemployment

Problems of being internationally uncompetitive

A fall in international competitiveness is likely to be reflected in a deterioration in the trade in goods balance of the balance of payments. In turn, this could result in an increase in unemployment, especially in industries in which exports are significant. A fall in exports could have a negative multiplier effect on GDP, so causing a reduction in economic growth.

Knowledge check 11

What would happen to international competitiveness if a country's productivity increased at a slower rate than that of its major competitors?

Examination skills and concepts

- Understanding the growing interdependence between economies.
- Ability to differentiate between the costs and benefits of globalisation.
- Ability to explain the basis of free trade in terms of the law of comparative advantage.
- Ability to use the tariff diagram to illustrate the implications of tariffs, including welfare losses.
- Evaluation of the possible conflicts between trading blocs and the WTO.
- Understanding the main components of the balance of payments accounts and being able to assess the impact on these components of changes in external factors (e.g. an increase in foreign direct investment).
- Understanding fixed, floating and managed exchange rates.
- Ability to analyse the effect of changes in the exchange rate on other macroeconomic variables.
- Assessing the case for and against membership of the eurozone.
- Understanding different measures of competitiveness.
- Factors influencing international competitiveness.

Common examination errors

- Confusion between absolute and comparative advantage.
- Imprecise diagrammatic analysis, especially in the case of tariffs.
- Misinterpreting trading blocs as protectionist measures.
- Confusion between a balance of payments deficit and a fiscal deficit.
- Confusion over the difference between components of the current account and components of the financial account.
- A lack of clarity in explaining the effects of a change in the exchange rate on the current account of the balance of payments and on the pattern of trade.
- Assuming that countries and groups such as the USA, EU and UK can 'devalue' or 'revalue' their currencies.
- Confusion between production and productivity.
- Confusion between the nominal and real exchange rate.

Links and common themes

- Application of opportunity cost (Theme 1) to the law of comparative advantage.
- Supply and demand analysis in considering tariffs and quotas (Theme 1).
- The balance of payments accounts (Theme 2).
- Causes of changes in exchange rates under a system of floating exchange rates: application of supply and demand analysis (Theme 1).
- Price elasticities of demand for imports and exports (Theme 1) when considering exchange rate changes.
- This section has close links with productivity, supply-side polices and the balance of payments (Theme 2).
- There are links with other parts of this theme, including the factors influencing growth in developing countries.

Summary

- Globalisation refers to the increased economic integration between countries through, for example, increased trade.
- Many factors have contributed to increased globalisation, including: the lowering of trade barriers; lower communication and transport costs; the opening up of China.
- Benefits of globalisation may be analysed using the law of comparative advantage and costs, using concepts such as external costs and increased inequality.
- The law of comparative advantage states that trade between two nations can be beneficial to both if each specialises in the production of a good with lower opportunity cost.
- The main roles of the WTO are to promote free trade and settle trade disputes.
- Trading blocs are groups of countries that trade freely among themselves but set trade barriers against non-members.
- Arguments for protectionism include: employment protection; prevention of dumping; protection of infant industries; retaliation.
- Protectionism may take several forms, such as tariffs, quotas, subsidies to domestic producers, and non-tariff barriers.
- The current account of the balance of payments is mainly concerned with the trade in goods and services between countries.

- The financial account is important when considering FDI and 'hot money' flows between countries.
- Current account deficits may be caused by factors including: a lack of competitiveness; an overvalued exchange rate; relatively low productivity; and non-price factors such as poor quality and design.
- Global imbalances arise when some countries have persistent current account deficits while others have persistent current account surpluses.
- In a free market, exchange rates are determined by the supply of and demand for currencies on the foreign exchange market.
- However, exchange rates may be fixed in relation to another currency or managed by the central bank through intervention in the foreign exchange market.
- A floating exchange rate may be affected by factors such as confidence; relative interest rates; relative inflation rates; and expectations about the future state of the economy.
- Revaluation or appreciation of a currency implies that its exchange rate has increased against other currencies.
- Devaluation or depreciation of a currency implies that its exchange rate has decreased against other currencies.

- A change in the exchange rate of a country's currency will affect a country's current account of the balance of payments, economic growth, unemployment, rate of inflation and FDI.
- International competitiveness reflects the ability of a country to sell its goods and services in world markets.
- The key factors influencing competitiveness are: relative unit labour costs; relative productivity rates; education and training; capital per worker; infrastructure; non-wage factors including national insurance contributions; and regulations, e.g. relating to the environment, and to health and safety.
- International competitiveness could be increased by supply-side policies or by a depreciation of the country's currency.

Poverty and inequality

Absolute and relative poverty

Absolute poverty

According to the World Bank, people are considered to be living in absolute poverty if their incomes fall below the minimum level to meet basic needs such as food, shelter, clothing, access to clean water, sanitation facilities, education and information. This minimum level is usually called the *poverty line*.

One of the key Millennium Development Goals was to halve the number of people living in absolute poverty by 2015. This target of reducing extreme poverty rates by half was met by 2010, when 700 million fewer people than in 1990 were living in conditions of extreme poverty. However, in 2015, 1.2 billion people were still living in extreme poverty. These Millennium Development Goals were succeeded by the Sustainable Development Goals in 2015, the first of which is to 'End poverty in all its forms everywhere'.

Relative poverty

People are considered to be in relative poverty if they are living below a certain income threshold in a particular country: for example, below 60% of the median income. Therefore, the concept of relative poverty is:

- subjective
- subject to change over time
- not comparable between countries (i.e. someone deemed relatively poor in the USA would be regarded as being incredibly rich in Malawi)

Relative poverty arises from inequality (see below).

Measures of absolute and relative poverty

Measure of absolute poverty

Absolute poverty is based on a set standard that is consistent over time and between countries, referring to the ability of individuals or groups to meet their basic needs.

In 2015, the World Bank set the international absolute poverty line at $1.90 a day at 2005 GDP measured at purchasing power parity, i.e. adjusted for international purchasing power.

Measure of relative poverty

Relative poverty is measured in comparison with other people in the country. Therefore, there will always be some people who are relatively poor in any given country. Relative poverty lines are defined in relation to the overall distribution of income or consumption in a country, so if a person is living below a certain income threshold in a particular country, they would be classified as being in relative poverty. For example, in the EU, people whose income is less than 60% of median income are considered to be 'at risk of poverty' and are said to be relatively poor.

> **Exam tip**
>
> All countries will have some people living in relative poverty because incomes are unevenly distributed. However, it is possible for a country to have no one living in absolute poverty because this is defined in terms of an internationally agreed measure.

> **Knowledge check 12**
>
> Will a fall in absolute poverty necessarily cause a fall in relative poverty?

Causes of changes in absolute and relative poverty

Changes in any of the following factors may result in changes in absolute and relative poverty:

- aid
- debt relief
- fair-trade schemes
- microfinance schemes
- employment opportunities
- education and training
- wage rates and national minimum wages
- property rights
- ownership of assets and their prices, e.g. houses and shares
- social benefits (transfer payments)

Inequality

Distinction between wealth and income inequality

Wealth is a *stock* concept. Wealth inequality refers to inequality based on value of tangible assets, e.g. property, shares, works of art.

Income, on the other hand, is a *flow* concept. Income inequality refers to inequality based on incomes from wages, rent and profit.

Measurements of income inequality: the Lorenz curve and the Gini coefficient

The Lorenz curve

The degree of inequality can be measured using a Lorenz curve, which plots the cumulative percentage of the population against the cumulative percentage of total income. The 45° line represents perfect equality such that the poorest 10% of the population would receive 10% of the income, the poorest 20% of the population would receive 20% of the income and so on. The curved line represents an unequal distribution of income. In Figure 7, the areas A and B are used in the calculation of the Gini coefficient (see below).

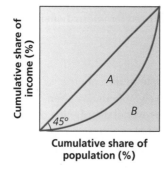

Figure 7 The Lorenz curve

Knowledge check 13

What would happen to the Lorenz curve if inequality within a country increased?

The Gini coefficient

This is a measure of the degree of inequality in a country. It is calculated as follows:

$$G = \frac{A}{A + B}$$

where A represents the area between the diagonal line and the Lorenz curve and B represents the area under the Lorenz curve. The Gini coefficient will have a value of between 0 and 1, with 0 representing absolute equality (i.e. the Lorenz curve and line of total equality are merged) and 1 absolute inequality (i.e. the Lorenz curve would lie along the horizontal and vertical axes). The Gini coefficient may also be expressed as a percentage:

$$G = \frac{A}{A + B} \times 100$$

Causes of income and wealth inequality

Inequality may be the result of a variety of factors, including:

- education and training
- wage rates
- unemployment
- social benefits (transfer payments)
- progressive and regressive taxes
- inheritance
- ownership of assets and their prices, e.g. houses and shares
- pensions (state and private)

Impact of economic change and development on inequality

Inequality is often regarded as an inevitable cost associated with economic growth because owners of resources and the means of production will become wealthier relative to workers. However, it may be argued that inequality itself is a constraint on economic change and development for the following reasons:

- The very poor will have no collateral and so will be unable to start their own businesses.
- Absolute poverty could remain high in countries where inequality is high.
- Those on low incomes will have a low marginal propensity to save, so limiting funds available for investment, while those on high incomes may spend a large amount of their incomes on imported goods or may transfer their incomes to other countries (known as *capital flight*; see page 38).

Further, there may be socially undesirable consequences of inequality, such as an increase in the crime rate, which might have an adverse effect on growth and development.

Significance of capitalism for inequality

The free market economy and capitalism were considered in Theme 1 where inequality was identified as one of the consequences of such an

> **Exam tip**
>
> Make sure that you can draw an accurately labelled Lorenz curve diagram and can show an increase or decrease in inequality.

economic system. The reason relates back to two key features of the free
market economy:

- private ownership of resources
- the profit motive

It is inevitable that private ownership of resources will enable those who accumulate
more assets to be richer relative to those who own few resources. The profit motive
is necessary in a capitalist, free market economy to encourage entrepreneurs to take
the risks involved in production. Such entrepreneurs are likely to become much richer
than workers if their businesses prove to be successful.

Examination skills and concepts

- Understanding the difference between absolute poverty and relative poverty.
- Understanding how absolute and relative poverty may be measured.
- Ability to explain the factors influencing income and wealth inequality.
- Understanding the Lorenz curve and the Gini coefficient.

Common examination errors

- Confusion between absolute and relative poverty.
- Confusion between income and wealth.
- Imprecision in drawing and labelling a Lorenz curve diagram.
- Failing to interpret the Lorenz curve and Gini coefficient correctly.

Links and common themes

- This section has links with the next section on emerging and developing
  countries, especially the factors influencing growth and development.

Summary

- Absolute poverty refers to people who have insufficient resources to meet their basic needs, whereas relative poverty refers to those living below a certain income level.
- Wealth and income inequality may be caused by a variety of factors, including: inheritance; ownership of assets; education; wage rates; age; pension entitlements; unemployment; taxes; and social benefits.
- Inequality may be measured by reference to the Lorenz curve and Gini coefficient.
- Inequality may limit growth and development, e.g. because those in absolute poverty will be unable to obtain loans to start businesses.

■ Emerging and developing economies

Measures of development

The human development index (HDI)

The HDI is a composite index of development and includes three elements:

- education (the mean years of schooling for an adult aged 25 and expected years of schooling for a pre-school child)
- health (life expectancy at birth)
- real GNI per head at purchasing power parities

This index results in a number between 0 and 1: the higher the value, the higher the level of development.

The inequality-adjusted HDI (IHDI)

The IHDI is published alongside the HDI and takes into account how human development is distributed. Countries which are very unequal see their human development scores fall more than those that are less unequal. Therefore, the difference between the HDI and the IHDI represents the 'loss' in potential human development due to inequality.

The multi-dimensional poverty index (MPI)

The global MPI is composed of ten indicators corresponding to the same three components as the HDI: education, health and standard of living. Multi-dimensional poverty is made up of several factors that constitute poor people's experience of deprivation — such as poor health, lack of education, inadequate living standard, disempowerment, poor quality of work and threat from violence.

Therefore, the global MPI combines two aspects of poverty:

- incidence, i.e. the percentage of people who are poor
- the intensity of people's poverty, i.e. the average of the components identified above in which poor people are deprived

Other indicators

These include:

- the proportion of the male population engaged in agriculture
- energy consumption per person
- the proportion of the population with access to clean water
- mobile phones per thousand of population
- the proportion of the population with internet access

Factors influencing growth and development

While all countries face constraints on their growth and development, there is an enormous difference in the scale of the constraints affecting developed and developing countries. Further, the particular problems facing different developing or developed countries vary considerably. It is important, therefore, to have some knowledge of specific countries in order to give relevant examples. This section and the next one focus primarily on problems facing developing countries (see Figure 8).

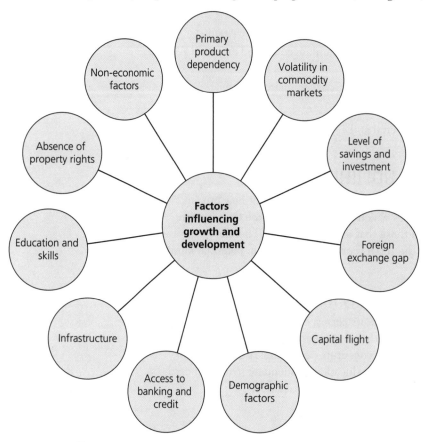

Figure 8 Factors influencing growth and development

Primary product dependency

Primary products may be divided into hard commodities, such as copper, tin and iron ore, and soft commodities, which include most agricultural crops, such as wheat, palm oil, rice and fruit. A range of issues face countries dependent on primary products, including the following:

- *Price fluctuations.* See page 36.
- *Difficulty of planning investment and output.* The price fluctuations cause uncertainty, which is a deterrent to investment.

- *Natural disasters.* Extreme weather such as hurricanes, tornadoes, droughts and tsunamis can cause severe disruption to the production of primary products, especially agricultural products.
- *Protectionism by developed countries.* For example, the huge subsidies given to US cotton farmers have created great difficulties for Indian cotton farmers, who are unable to compete; the EU's Common Agricultural Policy has meant that there is no free access to European markets for food from developing countries.
- *Low income elasticity of demand for primary products.* The Prebisch–Singer hypothesis states that the terms of trade between primary products and manufactured goods tend to deteriorate over time.

The Prebisch–Singer hypothesis

This theory suggests that countries that export commodities would be able to import less and less for a given level of exports. Prebisch and Singer examined data over a long period of time and found the data suggested that the terms of trade for primary commodity exporters *did* have a tendency to decline. A common explanation for this is that the income elasticity of demand for manufactured goods is greater than that for primary products, especially food. Therefore, as incomes rise, the demand for manufactured goods increases more rapidly than demand for primary products and the prices of manufactured goods rise relative to the prices of primary products, so causing a decline in the terms of trade for countries dependent on the export of primary products.

The theory may be criticised on the following grounds.
- First, some countries have developed on the basis of their primary products (e.g. Botswana: diamonds).
- Second, if a developing country has a comparative advantage in a primary product, then its resources will be used more efficiently by specialising in the production of that product.
- Third, primary product prices rose sharply until the middle of 2008 while the prices of many manufactured products were falling.

Some economists argue that, in the case of food, prices are likely to increase as world population grows and incomes in countries such as China and India rise, so causing higher demand for many foods traditionally eaten by those in developed countries.

Similarly, the outlook for countries such as Bolivia is good. Nearly half the world's known reserves of lithium (which can be used to make batteries for hybrid and electric vehicles) are located in Bolivia. Given the decline in oil production, and the subsidies being given to companies to develop electric cars, demand for lithium can be expected to rise sharply in the future.

In contrast, countries producing and exporting copper, such as Chile, were faced with a 50% fall in price between the middle of 2008 and 2009.

Volatility in commodity markets

Demand for, and supply of, commodities tend to be price inelastic. In the case of demand, this is because they are required in the production of other goods for which demand is also price inelastic, such as pasta, bread and steel. Supply is inelastic

Knowledge check 14

Why is the demand for most primary products income inelastic?

Exam tip

Always be prepared to include some theoretical models in your analysis. Evaluation is then possible by reference to real examples.

because a long growing period is required for soft commodities (most agricultural commodities) while for hard commodities, e.g. coal and diamonds, considerable time is required for developing new mines. Consequently, any demand-side or supply-side shock will result in a significant price change. In turn, price changes will result in fluctuations in producers' incomes and foreign exchange earnings. For example, since demand is price inelastic, then a fall in price will cause total revenue to fall and, therefore, the foreign currency earnings from exports to fall.

Any shift in the supply curve or the demand curve would cause a sharp change in price. A shift in the supply curve of an agricultural commodity might occur if there is a drought, while an earthquake might disrupt the production of copper mining. Since demand is price inelastic, then a leftward shift in the supply curve would cause a significant increase in price.

Figure 9 shows the effect on the price of wheat of both a leftward shift in the supply curve, e.g. caused by a drought, and a rightward shift in the supply curve, e.g. caused by a bumper harvest.

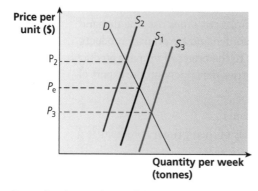

Figure 9 The effect of a change in conditions of supply on the price of wheat

The diagram (Figure 9) shows that shifts in the supply curve would cause a significant price rise when there is a decrease in supply and a significant price fall when there is an increase in supply.

Similarly, a change in the conditions of demand would cause a significant price change because supply is price inelastic. Demand has increased for a number of reasons, including:

- an increase in world population, which is now over 7 billion
- an increase in real incomes, which has led to increased demand for many commodities (for example, the demand for beef, which requires large amounts of grain for animal feed, has increased significantly)
- an increased demand for grain to be used for fuel

Level of savings and investment

Many developing countries a have low GDP per capita and consequently they hold inadequate savings to finance the investment seen as essential to achieve economic growth and development. The Harrod–Domar model, shown in Figure 10, illustrates the problem.

Knowledge check 15

Is the value of the marginal propensity to save likely to be high or low in poor countries?

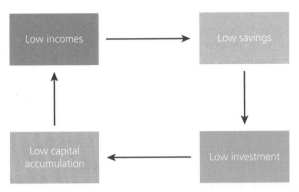

Figure 10 Low GDP per capita and the savings gap

Foreign exchange gap

Associated with the savings gap, many developing countries face a shortage of foreign exchange. This may be the result of a variety of factors, including:

- dependence on export earnings from primary products
- dependence on imports of capital goods and other manufactured goods
- capital flight (see below)
- debt

Debt is a particular problem for some emerging and developing countries and has become an issue for some developed countries, for example Greece, since the financial crisis. Many developing countries borrowed money at times of low interest rates, only to find that they were struggling to service the debt (pay the interest on it) some years later.

Debt has become a problem for a variety of reasons, including:

- risky decisions to borrow money to finance major investment projects at times when the world economy was strong and/or the prices of the goods which they were exporting were high
- an increase in oil prices, which presented particular problems over the periods of such price increases
- a fall in the value of the currencies of developing countries, which increased the burden of foreign debt
- loans taken out to finance expenditure on military equipment

When considering debt, it is important to remember that the absolute size of the debt is less important than a country's ability to finance it. This may be measured by examining data on debt service payments as a percentage of GDP or debt service payments as a percentage of export earnings.

Capital flight

This occurs when individuals or companies decide to place cash deposits in foreign banks or buy shares or other assets in foreign countries. This has serious implications, for example:

- it contributes to the savings gap and foreign currency gap, and consequently...
- it restricts economic growth
- it reduces the tax base because the country loses any tax payable on these assets

> **Exam tip**
>
> Capital flight and interest payments on debt result in an outflow of foreign currency from the current account of the balance of payments, thus making it more difficult for developing countries to finance imports.

Demographic factors

Population growth is particularly rapid in some of the poorest countries of the world, such as Malawi and Mozambique. Meanwhile, population is falling in some developed countries, such as Italy and Germany.

Population growth may be analysed in relation to the views of Thomas Malthus, who predicted at the end of the eighteenth century that famine was inevitable because population grows in geometric progression, whereas food production grows in the form of an arithmetic progression. Although his predictions were proved to be incorrect for Britain in the nineteenth century, some economists believe that they are still relevant for some of the poorest developing countries. In these countries the growth of the population is greater than the growth in GDP, with the result that GDP per capita is falling.

Knowledge check 16

What will happen to a country's dependency ratio if the birth rate remains high but the death rate decreases?

Access to credit and banking

Inability to borrow money is obviously important for both entrepreneurs who wish to start up new businesses and existing firms that may need credit to fund the purchase of capital and raw materials to operate effectively.

In some developing economies, banking services are poor or almost non-existent. However, *microfinance schemes* have helped to provide extremely poor families with small loans (microcredit) to help them engage in productive activities or grow their tiny businesses. In particular, they can help the poor to increase income, build businesses and reduce vulnerability to external shocks. For more on microfinance finance schemes, see page 42.

Infrastructure

Infrastructure covers the whole range of structures that are essential for an economy to operate smoothly. Infrastructure includes:

- transport
- telecommunications
- energy supply
- water supply
- waste disposal

Poor infrastructure will make it difficult to attract both domestic and foreign investment and thus presents a significant obstacle to growth and development. On the other hand, a country rich in a natural resource demanded by other countries might benefit from foreign direct investment: a transnational company might provide some infrastructure to the country in order to facilitate its business investment, e.g. new roads, thus benefiting the whole country.

Education and skills

A country whose education standards are poor and where there is a low school enrolment ratio is likely to experience a slow rate of economic growth because the productivity of the workforce will be low. It will also act as a deterrent to global (transnational) companies to invest in the country because of the costs involved in educating and training workers.

A particular problem for some countries is the prevalence of HIV and AIDS; when an adult develops AIDS, he or she may be forced to give up work. This means that the children might be withdrawn from school, either because the school fees can no longer be afforded or because the children are required to work at home. A further problem arises if it is the teachers who contract AIDS, forcing them to give up work. The training of workers may also be disrupted by AIDS, particularly if a global company is involved and it decides that it is no longer profitable to operate in the country. The combined effect of these problems is to reduce the quantity and quality of education and training.

Absence of property rights

If individuals do not have property (ownership) rights, e.g. over land or property, then this might act as a constraint on economic growth and development. The reason is that, without any form of collateral, they would find it difficult to secure a bank loan which they might require to start a business.

Non-economic factors

Corruption, poor governance, wars and political instability

Corruption is usually defined as the use of power for personal gain. It may take a variety of forms, including bribery, extortion and diversion of resources to the governing elite. Corruption acts as a constraint on development when it causes an inefficient allocation of resources.

Poor governance implies that the rulers of a country have adopted policies that result in the country's resources being allocated inefficiently. Government failure (where government intervention results in a net welfare loss) might also be evident as part of poor governance.

Civil wars, such as those that have occurred in Sudan and the Democratic Republic of the Congo, disrupt growth and development. Indeed, in so far as they actually cause destruction of infrastructure and the death of many people, they might negate any progress made in previous years.

Similarly, *political instability* results in a considerable degree of uncertainty, which does not provide a sound basis on which businesses can operate.

All the above issues can deter both domestic investment and foreign direct investment and so limit the possibilities for growth and development.

Further, geography may have a significant impact on a country's ability to develop. For example, economic development is limited in a land-locked country such as Niger because of isolation from world markets resulting from high transportation costs.

Strategies influencing growth and development

A range of strategies may be used to promote growth and development but there is no one simple prescription: each country is individual, having a different history, geography and natural resources. Consequently, policies which may appear to have worked in one country will not necessarily be successful in another country.

Knowledge check 17

Why might an absence of property rights restrict growth and development?

Exam tip

It is very useful to have case study examples to include in your answers to illustrate these constraints on growth and development.

In practice, it is likely that a combination of strategies may be required, with the particular blend being dependent on the characteristics and needs of that country. Various strategies are outlined below. As with the previous section, the emphasis is on developing countries but some of the strategies described may also be relevant to developed economies. Figure 11 summarises these strategies.

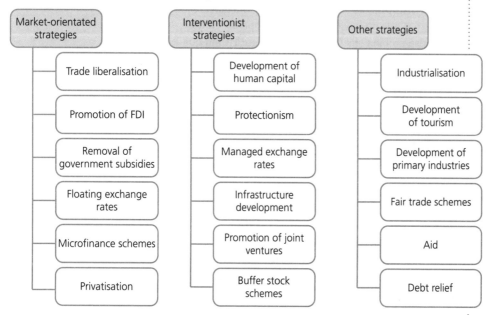

Figure 11 Strategies influencing growth and development

Market-orientated strategies

These strategies work through the operation of market forces. They usually involve measures to remove government intervention.

Trade liberalisation

Trade liberalisation refers to the lowering or complete removal of trade barriers such as tariffs, quotas and non-tariff barriers. Countries that have had sustained growth and prosperity have opened up their markets to trade and investment. By liberalising trade and focusing on areas of comparative advantage, countries can benefit economically. The effect of a reduction in tariffs on a particular country is illustrated in Figure 12.

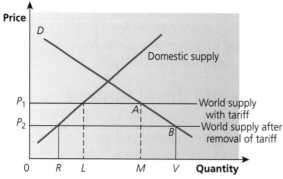

Figure 12 Effect of a reduction in tariffs

When tariffs are reduced, the world price falls from P_1 to P_2, resulting in an increase in consumer surplus of P_2P_1AB. Imports will increase from LM to RV.

The benefits of trade liberalisation include the following:

- *Consumers* benefit because liberalised trade can help to lower prices and increase the choice and quality of goods and services available.
- *Companies* can benefit because liberalised trade diversifies risks and enables firms to benefit from economies of scale, resulting in lower long-run average costs.
- A *country's economy* may benefit from trade liberalisation because it promotes competition, and usually leads to increased investment and productivity.

The OECD has estimated that if G20 economies reduced trade barriers by 50%, then there would be:

- *Increased employment:* for example, a 0.3–3.3% rise in jobs for lower-skilled workers and a 0.9–3.9% rise for higher-skilled workers, depending on the country.
- *Higher real wages:* an increase in real wages of 1.8–8% for lower-skilled workers and 0.8–8.1% for higher-skilled workers, depending on the country.
- *Increased exports:* all G20 countries would see a boost in exports. In the long run, many G20 countries could see their exports rise by 20% and those in the eurozone by more than 10%.

On the other hand, trade liberalisation may have drawbacks, as listed below.

- It may negatively affect some industries or some jobs.
- It has adverse effects on the environment (external costs associated with trade).
- It may negatively affect infant industries in developing and emerging economies.

Knowledge check 18

Why might trade liberalisation be resisted by some developing countries?

Exam tip

Trade liberalisation implies the removal of trade barriers and you should be able to assess the advantages and disadvantages of such policies for developing countries.

Promotion of FDI

Foreign direct investment is viewed as being desirable because it acts as an injection into the circular flow, provides employment opportunities, and increases the productive potential of the economy. Therefore, governments may try to promote FDI in a variety of ways, including:

- reduction in corporation tax
- tax incentives and grants
- reduction in bureaucracy, e.g. easing of planning regulations
- liberalisation of labour laws, e.g. ease of hiring and firing workers; zero hours contracts
- reducing trade barriers so that it is easier to import components and to export finished goods

Removal of government subsidies

Subsidies distort the operation of market forces and are likely to result in a misallocation of resources. Governments in India, Egypt and Indonesia have been trying to cut food and energy subsidies because of their cost and the distorting effects which they have on their economies.

Floating exchange rates

Allowing the exchange rate of a currency to float might result in a depreciation against other currencies, so making the country's goods and services more competitive. This might encourage global companies to invest in that country since the currency is no longer overvalued.

Microfinance schemes

Microfinance is a means of providing extremely poor families with small loans (microcredit) to help them engage in productive activities or grow their tiny businesses. It can help the poor to increase income, build businesses and reduce vulnerability to external shocks. The pioneer of microfinance was Muhammad Yunus, who established the Grameen Bank in Bangladesh.

The key features of microfinance schemes are as follows:

- Microcredit insists on repayment (in contrast to development aid).
- Interest is charged to cover the costs involved.
- The focus is on groups whose alternative sources of finance are limited to the informal sector, where the interest charged would be high.

The main clients of microfinance are:

- women (who form more than 97% of the clients)
- the self-employed, often household-based entrepreneurs
- small farmers in rural areas
- small shopkeepers, street vendors and service providers in urban areas

Despite some obvious successes, microfinance have been criticised on several grounds:

- Concerns have been raised about the repayment rate, collection methods and questionable accounting practices.
- On a larger scale, some argue that an overemphasis on microfinance to combat poverty will lead to a reduction of other assistance to the poor, such as official development assistance or aid from non-government organisations (NGOs).

Privatisation

The sale of publicly owned assets to the private sector through the issue of shares has been a popular policy in developed economies for many years and has also been adopted by some developing countries. Privatisation is seen as a way of increasing efficiency and productivity as a result of competition and the profit motive, which are characteristics of the private sector.

Interventionist strategies

These strategies involve intervention by the state in order to influence the allocation of resources. Various forms of intervention are considered on the following pages.

Development of human capital

Countries with poor education standards and low school enrolment ratios are likely to experience slow rates of economic growth. Therefore, improvements in access to education and in the quality of education would help to increase the skills and productivity of the workforce. Such improvements would also encourage FDI by global companies in these countries.

Protectionism

This strategy is aimed at constructing a path towards diversification and industrialisation. Its characteristics include placing controls on imported goods, e.g. tariffs and quotas. This helps to promote *import substitution* (i.e. replacement of imports with domestically produced manufactured goods). It is sometimes referred to as an *inward-looking strategy*.

The aim of protectionism is to enable a country to diversify in a controlled way until it has built a strong domestic base. This approach will be most effective where a country's domestic market is large enough to enable industries to benefit from economies of scale. Once achieved, industry will be strong enough to cope with foreign competition.

However, there are some drawbacks to this approach:
■ *Comparative advantage* is distorted and so resources will not be allocated efficiently.
■ The *lack of competition* could result in inefficiency.

Managed exchange rates

Some countries try to maintain overvalued exchange rates with the aim of keeping down the cost of imports, especially of oil and capital equipment. In turn, this would make it easier for them to grow and develop.

Infrastructure development

Infrastructure refers to the physical and organisational structures and facilities, such as buildings, roads, railways, power supplies and the internet, needed for the operation of a society or enterprise. Without these it would be difficult for a country to grow and develop.

Promotion of joint ventures

A joint venture is an association of two or more businesses for the purpose of engaging in a specific enterprise for profit. Firms might enter into joint ventures to combine strengths and increase their competitive advantage while minimising risks.

Examples:
■ In 2012, Jaguar Land Rover sealed a joint venture with Chinese company Chery Automobile for the purpose of manufacturing and distributing luxury cars to Chinese consumers.
■ Kellogg Company entered into a joint venture agreement with Wilmar International Limited for the purpose of selling and distributing cereal and snack foods to consumers in China.

Buffer stock schemes

One method of reducing price stability is to adopt schemes which involve storing and releasing the commodity in times of surplus and shortage. The following analysis describes one way by which a **buffer stock scheme** might operate.

- A ceiling price: this is the maximum price which would be allowed.
- A floor price: this is the minimum price which would be allowed.
- A buffer stock would be established: this could be operated either by a government or by a producers' association. It would store or release stocks as required in order to reduce price fluctuations to the agreed limits.

Figure 13 illustrates the operation of a buffer stock scheme.

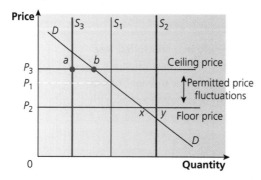

Figure 13 The operation of a buffer stock scheme

- In year 1, the equilibrium price is P_1 so no action is required because the price is within the permitted price range.
- Suppose supply is S_2 in year 2, then, to prevent the price from falling below the floor price, xy would be removed from the market and stored in a buffer stock.
- If supply fell to S_3 in year 3, then, to prevent the price rising above the ceiling level, ab would be released from the buffer stock.

Critique of buffer stock schemes

In practice, many problems are associated with these schemes:

- If the floor price is set too high, then there will be surpluses each year.
- Equally, if the ceiling price is set too low, then there may be insufficient stocks available in years of shortage.
- The schemes involve costs of storage.
- Success depends on ensuring that all the major producers agree to be part of the scheme and that none of them cheats, e.g. by selling to a major consumer at a reduced price.

Other strategies

Industrialisation: the Lewis model

It has traditionally been assumed that development is synonymous with industrialisation, i.e. that development requires an increasingly large manufacturing sector. The structural change/dual sector model (the *Lewis model*) is based on the view that development requires a move away from traditional agriculture

Exam tip

The analysis is more straightforward if the supply is assumed to be perfectly inelastic. This is a reasonable assumption because a set amount will be produced each year.

Knowledge check 19

Give two examples of market-orientated strategies and two examples of interventionist strategies to promote growth and development.

(characterised by subsistence, low productivity and barter) to more productive manufacturing (characterised by high productivity and monetary exchange).

Key features of the Lewis model

- This model describes the transfer of surplus labour from a low productivity (subsistence) agricultural sector to a high productivity industrial sector.
- Lewis thought that, because of the excess supply of workers, the marginal productivity (MP) of agricultural workers might be zero or close to zero. This is based on the **law of diminishing returns**.
- With MP at zero, then the opportunity cost of transferring workers from the agricultural sector to the industrial sector would be zero.
- Industrialisation will be associated with investment (possibly from global companies), which will increase productivity and profitability. If profits are reinvested, then further growth will occur.
- The share of profits as a percentage of GDP will increase, as will the savings ratio, providing more funds for investment and continued economic growth.

Law of diminishing returns This states that, when successive units of a variable factor of production are added to fixed factors, the marginal product will eventually decrease.

Criticisms of the Lewis model

- Profits made in the industrial sector might not be invested locally, especially if firms are owned by transnational companies.
- Reinvestment might be made in capital equipment, with the result that extra labour is not required.
- Empirical evidence suggests that the assumption of surplus labour in the agricultural sector and full employment in the industrial sector is invalid, e.g. favelas in South America.

Development of tourism

Some countries have developed on the basis of investment in tourism. There are advantages to this strategy over primary product dependency, not least that demand is likely to be *income elastic*. The expansion of tourism has strong attractions for developing countries, such as Kenya and the Maldives.

Advantages associated with the development of tourism

- It is a valuable source of foreign currency as tourists spend money on goods and services provided within the local economy.
- Tourism is likely to attract investment by transnational hotel chains.
- In turn, this will increase GDP via the multiplier.
- Jobs will be created, both as a direct result of the investment in the tourist and leisure industries and also as a result of the multiplier effects within the economy.
- All of the above will help to increase tax revenues for the government, which may be used to improve public services.
- It can help to preserve the national heritage of the country.
- Improvements in infrastructure may be made (e.g. a transnational company provides new roads as part of its contract to build hotels).

Disadvantages associated with tourism

- It may be associated with a significant increase in imports, not only for the capital equipment required to build hotels and facilities but also to meet the demands of tourists for specialist foods and goods. Further, the balance of payments on current account might be adversely affected by the repatriation of profits to shareholders of TNCs.

- In times of recession, demand may fall proportionately more than the fall in real income, assuming that demand is income elastic.
- Employment may only be seasonal in nature. Further, the jobs created may only be low skilled and low paid if the TNC supplies its own managers and professional staff.
- Tourism is subject to changes in fashion. In the developed world, Spain has suffered from a significant downturn in tourism in recent years, as Europeans now prefer more exotic destinations.
- There may be significant *external costs* (e.g. increase in waste, pollution of beaches, water shortages for local people) as the needs of tourists are prioritised. The damage to the environment caused by tourists might result in restrictions (e.g. the restrictions on the number of tourists allowed each day on the Galápagos islands; visitors to Machu Picchu are limited by the requirement to have a guide).

Development of primary industries

Some developing countries have achieved growth and development on the basis of investing in primary industries. The case for focusing on agriculture and hard commodities is that the country may have a comparative advantage in the production of these goods and so resources are more efficiently allocated to that use. Such a comparative advantage should be viewed in a dynamic context (i.e. as the country experiences growth, the government may use its tax revenues to spend on education). As a result of such a dynamic, the country may gain a comparative advantage in other products.

Some countries have specialised in producing primary products with a high income elasticity of demand, e.g. Peru produces asparagus; Chile produces blueberries, wine and papaya; Bolivia produces tin. Consequently, during periods of world economic growth, they have benefited from significant increases in demand.

Fair trade schemes

The aim of fair trade schemes is 'to address the injustice of low prices' by guaranteeing that producers receive a fair price. It means paying producers an above-market price for their produce, provided they meet particular labour and production standards. This premium is passed back to the producers to spend on development programmes.

The market for fair trade products has been growing rapidly and there are now over 2,500 product lines, including chocolate, tea, coffee, bananas, wine and clothes.

Advantages of fair trade schemes

- Producers receive a higher price.
- Extra money is available to spend on education, health, infrastructure, clean water supplies, conversion to organic farming and other development programmes in the producers' countries.

Knowledge check 20

Name two countries in which tourism has been a significant factor in influencing growth and development.

- There are smaller price fluctuations, allowing producers to be shielded from market forces.
- The extra money can also be used to improve the quality of products.
- Producers are enabled to diversify into other products.

Criticisms of fair trade schemes

- Distortion of market forces: low prices are due to overproduction and producers ought to recognise this as a signal to switch to growing other crops. Further, the artificially high prices encourage more producers to enter the market.
- Certification is based on normative views on the best way to organise labour, e.g. in the case of coffee, certification is only available to cooperatives of small producers.
- Guaranteeing a minimum price provides no incentive to improve quality.
- It is an inefficient way to get money to poor producers: consumers pay a large premium for fair trade goods but much of this goes to supermarkets in profits. Only 10% of the premium paid for fair trade coffee trickles down to the producer.
- The schemes may create a dependency trap for producers.

Aid

The term 'aid' is used to describe the voluntary transfer of resources from one country to another or to loans given on concessionary terms (i.e. at less than the market rate of interest). Official development assistance relates specifically to aid provided by governments and it excludes aid given by voluntary agencies. Aid may also be given for emergency relief (e.g. in the case of natural disasters or for the support of refugees during a civil war). This kind of aid is not usually contentious and so the focus here is on aid given for more general purposes. The UN goal for the amount of aid offered by developed countries (agreed in 1970) is 0.7% of GDP.

There are various types of aid:

- *Tied aid.* This is aid with conditions attached (e.g. there might be a requirement to buy goods from the donor country or the aid might be given on condition that there are some economic and political reforms).
- *Bilateral aid.* This is aid given directly by one country to another.
- *Multilateral aid.* This occurs when countries pay money to an international agency which then distributes it to countries on the basis of certain criteria.

The arguments in favour of aid include the following:

- The reduction in absolute poverty.
- Filling the savings gap experienced by many developing countries (this may be related to the Harrod–Domar model).
- Providing funds for infrastructure — essential if the country is to industrialise. Aid, therefore, will help to increase aggregate demand and investment will have a multiplier effect on GDP. In turn, this will help to promote sectoral development.
- Improving human capital through promotion of healthcare, education, training and expertise (e.g. the training of teachers and doctors). In some countries, aid might be used to help the prevention and treatment of AIDS.
- Possible contribution to increased globalisation and trade, both of which are frequently associated with growth and development.
- The reduction of world inequality.

Knowledge check 21

What is the difference between aid and FDI?

There are powerful arguments against the use of aid, except in the case of emergency aid, some of which are listed below:

- It results in a dependency culture (i.e. the recipients of aid become dependent on it and do not therefore pursue appropriate macroeconomic policies to achieve independent growth and development).
- Aid might not benefit those for whom it is intended (e.g. it could be diverted into military expenditure or it could be 'lost' as a result of corruption).
- There is no clear evidence that aid contributes to the reduction of absolute poverty or to growth and development.
- Right-wing economists argue that aid distorts market forces and results in an inefficient allocation of resources, while left-wing economists regard aid as a form of economic imperialism by which donor countries aim to secure political influence in the countries to which they give aid.
- Aid in the form of concessional loans involves the repayment of interest, in which case there will be an opportunity cost for the developing countries, e.g. improvements in the health and education services.

Debt relief

The burden of debt bears heavily on some countries, e.g. the Gambia, Mali, Nicaragua, Bolivia and Malawi.

The debt is usually owed to all or some of the following: the IMF, the World Bank, governments and banks in the developed countries.

The problem is that servicing the debt may account for a disproportionate amount of public expenditure, to the extent that resources available for expenditure on health and education are severely limited. As a result, pressure to cancel the debts of the poorest countries has increased.

Under the Heavily Indebted Poor Countries (HIPC) initiative and the Multilateral Debt Relief Initiative (MDRI), the World Bank provides debt relief to the poorest countries of the world. The HIPC initiative was started in 1996 by the IMF and World Bank with the aim of reducing the external debts of the poorest and most heavily indebted countries of the world to sustainable levels. Changes were made in 1999 to make the process quicker and deeper and to strengthen the links between debt relief poverty reduction and social policies.

In 2005, the HIPC initiative was enhanced by the MDRI in order to speed up progress towards meeting the Millennium Development Goals (MDGs). Forty-one countries were identified as being eligible for HIPC initiative assistance and by the end of 2015, 36 countries had benefited from HIPC debt relief.

Knowledge check 22

What is meant by debt servicing and why is it significant?

Arguments for debt cancellation

- Developing countries would have more foreign currency with which to buy imported capital and consumer goods from the developed countries.
- To the extent that the money released from debt cancellation is used for the purchase of capital goods, then there is the prospect of higher economic growth in the future.
- In turn, this means that developing countries would be able to buy more goods from richer countries.

- It would help to reduce absolute poverty.
- It would help to reduce both the savings gap and the foreign exchange gap.
- It might help to conserve the environment, e.g. 'debt for nature swaps'.

Arguments against the cancellation of debt

- In comparison with aid, it is likely to take much longer to agree a debt cancellation programme.
- Unless conditions are attached to debt cancellation, there is no guarantee that the governments of these countries will pursue sound macroeconomic policies (i.e. there is a moral hazard problem).
- Corruption might mean that the benefits of debt cancellation are channelled to government officials rather than to the poor.
- Shareholders of banks in the developed world may bear some of the burden of debt cancellation.
- It may be much less effective than the introduction of policies to reduce protectionism in developed countries.

Awareness of international institutions and non-government organisations (NGOs)

World Bank — the International Bank for Reconstruction and Development (IBRD)

The original role of the World Bank was to provide long-term loans for reconstruction and development to member nations that had suffered in the Second World War.

In the 1970s, its role changed to setting up agricultural reforms in developing countries, giving loans and providing expertise.

In 1982, Mexico defaulted on its loan repayments. As a result, the World Bank now imposes *structural adjustment programmes* (SAPs), which set out the conditions on which loans are given. The aim is to ensure that debtor countries do not default on the repayment of debts.

SAPs were based on free market reforms (e.g. trade liberalisation, removal of state subsidies on food, privatisation and reduction in public expenditure to reduce budget deficits). However, these free market reforms were criticised because they:

- did little to help the world's poor
- failed to promote development
- increased inequality
- caused environmental degradation
- resulted in social and political chaos in many countries

The widespread criticism of SAPs and the devastating effect which they had on some developing countries resulted in the World Bank changing its focus to concentrate on poverty reduction strategies, with aid being directed towards:

- countries following sound macroeconomic policies
- healthcare
- broadening education
- local communities rather than central governments

Exam tip

The arguments for and against debt cancellation are very similar to those for aid.

Knowledge check 23

Why might there be a moral hazard problem if debts of developing countries are cancelled?

Exam tip

Use case study material in your examination answers. The World Bank website (www.worldbank.org) provides detailed information on countries.

International Monetary Fund (IMF)

The original role of the International Monetary Fund was to increase international liquidity and to provide stability in capital markets through a system of convertible currencies pegged to the dollar. It also lent to countries with temporary balance of payments deficits on current account.

In the 1970s, there were significant oil price shocks and many countries — especially developing countries — suffered from rapid inflation, huge balance of payments deficits and debt crises. As a result, most currencies were allowed to float (i.e. the peg to the dollar was broken). The IMF extended its role to include involvement in economic development and poverty reduction. To ensure repayment of loans, the IMF imposed restrictions and conditions on the economic policies to be followed by developing countries — *stabilisation programmes* — to achieve internal and external balance. In practice, these were similar to *structural adjustment programmes* (see page 49).

In 2006, the IMF was given a new role; namely, to conduct multilateral surveillance of the global economy and to suggest steps that the leading nations should take to promote it. It was also required to ensure more balanced growth and to reduce global imbalances.

The IMF is funded by quotas from countries, based on their GDP. Up to a quarter of the quota is payable in dollars, euros, yen or sterling or *special drawing rights* (SDR) and the other three-quarters in the country's own currency. The value of an SDR is defined as the value of a fixed amount of yen, dollars, pounds and euros, expressed in dollars at the current exchange rate. These SDRs represent a potential claim on other countries' foreign currency reserves, for which they can be exchanged voluntarily. In December 2010, it was agreed that the IMF's quota resources would be doubled in order to deal with expected new demands resulting from the sovereign debt crisis.

The IMF can also borrow on the basis of the 'New Arrangements to Borrow' and the 'General Agreement to Borrow'. These provide the possibility of accessing about $580 billion in the event of a major financial crisis.

The future of the World Bank and the IMF

The roles of the IMF and the World Bank are currently blurred: both have a role in the developing world and in poverty reduction and it is suggested that they should be reformed to reflect the changing needs of the global economy. Critics of the institutions as they currently operate suggest the following:

■ The IMF should be slimmed down and should undertake short-term lending to crisis-hit countries.
■ The World Bank should act as a development agency and undertake a detailed appraisal of the creditworthiness of recipient countries.

NGOs

The work of non-government organisations (NGOs) has brought *community-based development* to the forefront of strategies to promote growth and development (i.e. the focus has moved away from state-managed schemes). The key characteristics of these community-based schemes are:

Knowledge check 24

What has been the role of the IMF in helping countries with sovereign debt crises?

- local control of small-scale projects
- self-reliance
- emphasis on using the skills available
- environmental sustainability

Examination skills and concepts

- Understanding the complex nature of economic development and its distinction from economic growth.
- Understanding the different ways by which development might be measured.
- Assessment of the significance of factors influencing growth and development with particular reference to concepts such as the savings gap, the foreign exchange gap, capital flight and primary product dependency.
- Ability to evaluate a range of strategies to promote growth and development and ability to differentiate between market-orientated strategies and interventionist strategies.
- Ability to give examples from specific countries to illustrate the points made. This skill may be gained by adopting a case-study approach.
- Evaluation of the roles of the IMF, the World Bank and NGOs.

Common examination errors

- Confusion between growth and development.
- Not providing examples to illustrate the point being made.
- Confusion between aid and FDI.
- Assumption that measures to increase economic growth will automatically result in development.

Links and common themes

- Primary product dependency may be illustrated using supply and demand analysis covered in Theme 1. Further, analysis of this issue involves the application of price elasticities of demand and supply and also income elasticity of demand.
- The significance of education and training was considered as a supply-side policy in Theme 2.
- In discussing the strategies, it is often appropriate to employ *AD/AS* analysis, e.g. in considering the impact of aid (see Theme 2).
- The market-orientated strategies link with the market economics covered in Theme 1.

Content Guidance

Summary

- There are several ways of measuring development such as the human development index (HDI).
- There are many factors that might influence growth and development in developing countries, one of the most significant of which is primary product dependency. This may be analysed by reference to the Prebisch–Singer hypothesis.
- Other factors affecting growth and development include: insufficient saving and foreign currency; fluctuations in commodity prices; capital flight; population issues; debt; access to credit and banking; education and skills; and unallocated property rights.
- Non-economic factors influencing growth and development include corruption, wars and political instability.
- There are many ways by which developing countries could achieve growth and development, including: market-orientated strategies, e.g. trade liberalisation, floating exchange rates and privatisation; interventionist strategies, e.g. protectionism, managed exchange rates and buffer stock schemes; and other strategies, e.g. industrialisation, development of tourism, aid, debt relief and fair trade schemes.
- The IMF, World Bank and non-government organisations (NGOs) can play an important role in promoting growth and development.

■ The financial sector

Role of financial markets

To facilitate saving

A traditional role of the banks and other financial institutions, e.g. insurance companies and pension funds, is to provide facilities for individuals and firms to save, so enabling them to purchase goods at a later date.

To lend to businesses and individuals

A function of banks and other financial institutions is to provide credit. Without this facility, individuals and businesses may have cash flow problems.

To facilitate exchange

Transfers of money can be arranged easily when there is a fully developed banking and financial system. With the growth of online banking and smart debit cards, most such transfers now occur electronically.

To provide forward markets in currencies and commodities

The foreign currency and commodity markets provide forward markets for currencies and commodities so that traders can buy in advance, thereby reducing risks associated with the price volatility that often characterises such markets.

To provide a market for equities

Stock exchanges enable stocks and shares to be traded. This enables companies to raise money and provides an opportunity for investors to purchase shares.

Market failure in the financial sector

Asymmetric information

Financial markets and the products they deal with have become increasingly complex over recent years.

Externalities

Failure of financial institutions may have undesirable spillover effects (external costs) on third parties who are not directly involved in the financial sector. For example, the failure of a bank might result in bankruptcies for other businesses if the bank customers lose their deposits and can no longer pay bills to other businesses or if the bank failure results in a fall in sales of other businesses.

Externalities Costs or benefits to third parties not part of the transaction. If externalities exist, there would be a divergence between social costs/benefits and private costs/benefits.

Moral hazard

Before the financial crisis some bankers engaged in trading highly risky securities to enhance their bonuses, thinking that any risk would be borne by shareholders. In the event, the losses made were so great that some banks, such as RBS, had to rescued by the UK government. This could create a further moral hazard (and government failure) because banks might continue to engage in risky behaviour, knowing that they would be bailed out by the government if they were in danger of going bankrupt.

Speculation and market bubbles

Between 2000 and 2007, UK banks created £1 trillion, doubling the amount of money and debt in the economy, but only 8% of this went to business. Over half went to residential and commercial property and 32% to the financial sector. This extra money in the economy helped to fuel bubbles in the property markets and eventually debts related to these bubbles became unpayable.

Market rigging

In 2015, several major banks around the world were fined for manipulation of Libor, the global benchmark interest rate. For example, Deutsche Bank, Germany's largest bank, was fined a record $2.5bn for rigging Libor and was ordered to sack seven employees.

Also, Barclays was fined £1.5bn after rogue traders were caught manipulating foreign currency rates.

Role of central banks

Implementation of monetary policy

Central banks are usually responsible for controlling the cost and supply of money. In this role they set interest rates, and are responsible for asset purchases (quantitative easing) and sales.

Many central banks are now independent of their governments but may be required to make such decisions in relation to an inflation target.

Banker to the government

Most governments keep their accounts with the central bank of the country.

Banker to the banks

Central banks also provide banking facilities to the high street banks. In the UK all banks must keep an account with the Bank of England.

Role of regulation in the banking industry

Following the financial crisis, many central banks are responsible for enforcing new regulations designed to prevent the risk of banks requiring a bailout from their government. These regulations are incredibly complex. For example, the Basel III regulations are over 200 pages long.

Knowledge check 25

Outline the external costs which could result from the failure of a bank.

Exam tip

Refer back to work covered in Theme 1 on market failure and use this analysis in answering questions on market failure in the financial sector.

Some key regulations in the EU are:

- the requirement for banks to split their retail banking business from their investment banking activities
- an increase in the amount of capital

Examination skills and concepts

- Ability to understand the role of financial markets in the economy.
- Ability to assess market failure in the financial sector with particular reference to the banking sector.
- Ability to evaluate the functions of a central bank in a country.

Common examination errors

- Confusing the role of central banks and that of retail banks.
- Assumption that financial institutions are only concerned with lending.

Links and common themes

- The market failures identified are applications of the concepts introduced in Theme 1.
- Monetary policy was considered in some depth in Theme 2.
- Many central banks are required to meet an inflation target set by the government, also considered in Theme 2.

Summary

- The financial sector plays a crucial role in any economy, not least in facilitating savings and making credit available.
- The financial crisis illustrated that market failures may be associated with the financial sector.
- A central bank plays a pivotal role in implementing monetary policy and in overseeing the whole financial sector.

■ The role of the state in the macroeconomy

Public finance

Figure 14 shows the key elements of public finance.

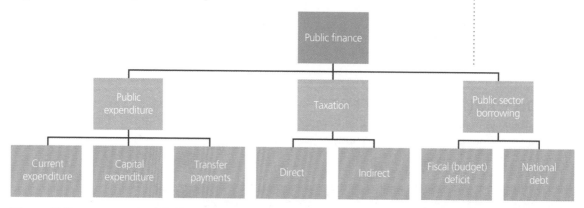

Figure 14 Key aspects of public finance

Public expenditure

Expenditure by central and local government can be categorised into three distinct types: capital expenditure, current expenditure and transfer payments.

Distinction between capital expenditure, current expenditure and transfer payments

Capital expenditure

This relates to expenditure on long-term investment projects such as new hospitals and roads. It is often referred to as *public sector investment*.

The objectives of public expenditure include the provision of public goods; defence and internal security; the provision of goods and services which yield external benefits and/or where there may be information gaps and asymmetric information, e.g. health and education; the redistribution of income; and expenditure to deal with external costs such as pollution and waste.

Current expenditure

This is day-to-day expenditure on goods and services, e.g. salaries of teachers and nurses and drugs used by the NHS.

Transfer payments

These are payments made by the state (from tax revenues) to individuals in the form of benefits for which there is no production in return. Examples include child benefit, state pensions and the jobseeker's allowance.

Knowledge check 26

What are the two key characteristics of public goods?

Exam tip

Transfer payments involve redistribution of income. Therefore they are not relevant to the calculation of a country's national income.

Reasons for the changing size and composition of public expenditure

Factors influencing the size and pattern of public expenditure include the following.

The level of GDP

As incomes increase, so do expectations, and the demand for many government-provided services such as health and education rises more than proportionately because demand for them is *income elastic*.

The size and age distribution of the population

An increase in the size of the population (e.g. through immigration) is likely to place extra pressure on public services, while an ageing population will increase demand for medical services and social services for the elderly.

Political priorities

A government in a developed country might place particular emphasis on improving the quality of health and education services, whereas the priority of a government in a developing country may be to improve infrastructure.

Redistribution of income

Expenditure on those in *relative poverty* (see page 29) and on those with disabilities increased significantly in many countries before the 2008 financial crisis. However, subsequent austerity measures aimed at reducing fiscal deficits have led to cuts in *means-tested benefits* such as tax credits and housing benefits, resulting in an increase in relative poverty.

Discretionary fiscal policy

The 2008 financial crisis led to the resurrection of fiscal policy as a means of macroeconomic management in many countries, although often only temporarily.

Debt interest

The massive increase in fiscal deficits from 2008 is leading to sharp rises in national debts in many countries. For example, Greece's national debt as a proportion of GDP increased from over 125% in 2009 to 180% in 2015. In turn, this results in higher interest payments so that less money is available for public services.

> **Exam tip**
>
> When answering questions on this area it is useful to have current knowledge of the reasons for recent changes in the size and pattern of public expenditure.

The significance of differing levels of public expenditure as a proportion of GDP

Productivity and growth

Public expenditure on areas such as education, infrastructure and health might cause an increase in productivity and so result in a rightward shift in the long-run aggregate supply curve.

An increase in public expenditure will also cause an increase in aggregate demand because it represents an injection into the circular flow and so will have a *multiplier effect* on GDP. Therefore, higher public expenditure would cause an increase in economic growth.

Living standards

Higher public expenditure as a proportion of GDP could result in an increase in living standards if, for example, much of it went to the improvement of public services such as health and education, or to housing and infrastructure. However, this would not necessarily be the case if most went on defence or on interest payments on the national debt.

Crowding out

Increased public expenditure could cause crowding out. This might take two forms: resource and financial.

- *Resource crowding out* occurs when the economy is operating at full employment and an increase in public expenditure results in insufficient resources being available for the private sector.
- *Financial crowding out* occurs when increased public expenditure or tax cuts are financed by increased public sector borrowing, so increasing the demand for loanable funds and driving up interest rates.

Level of taxation

Countries which have relatively low public expenditure as a proportion of GDP may also have relatively low levels of taxation. Some economists consider that this is desirable on the basis that the state is less efficient at allocating resources than the free market; that it gives consumers more choice in spending decisions; and that growth tends to be higher in countries in which public expenditure does not rise above 35% of GDP. However, Scandinavian countries have high living standards despite public expenditure being a relatively high proportion of GDP.

Equality

The impact of different levels of public expenditure on equality will also depend on the composition of that public expenditure. In countries in which public expenditure is weighted towards means-tested benefits, social housing, education, health and subsidies on basic food items, income distribution is likely to be more evenly distributed than in countries where public expenditure is weighted more to defence, universal benefits and prestigious investment projects.

Taxation

Distinction between progressive, proportional and regressive taxes

There are three broad categories of taxes: progressive, proportional and regressive.

Progressive tax

This is a tax in which the proportion of income paid in tax rises as income increases. Therefore, there are likely to be several tax bands, e.g. 10%, 20% and 45%, so that as income increases beyond a certain limit any further income is taxed at a higher tax rate.

Proportional tax

This is a tax in which the proportion of income paid in tax remains constant as income increases. For example, some countries, e.g. Latvia, Estonia and Hong Kong, have a flat rate of income tax.

Regressive tax

This is a tax in which the proportion of income paid in tax falls as income increases. Although governments do not deliberately set regressive taxes, some taxes have a regressive effect, most typically those on expenditure.

> **Exam tip**
>
> Remember that the distinction between these categories of taxes depends on the relationship between the percentage of income paid in tax and taxable income.

The distinction between direct and indirect taxes

	Direct taxes	Indirect taxes
What is being taxed?	Income and wealth	Expenditure
Where does the incidence of the tax fall, i.e. who bears the final burden of paying the tax?	A direct tax is paid by a person on whom it is legally imposed. Therefore, the burden of the tax cannot be shifted to any other person.	The burden of an indirect tax may be shifted in whole or in part from the person on whom it is imposed to a third party. For example, a business may be legally responsible for paying VAT but part or all of the burden may be passed on to consumers. Analysis of this was covered in Theme 1.
Examples?	Income tax, capital gains tax, corporation tax	Value added tax, excise duties, tariffs

The economic effects of changes in direct tax rates

Incentives to work

An increase in tax rates might have significant disincentive effects. For example, if the basic rate of income tax were raised, there would be less incentive for the unemployed or those not currently participating in the workforce to accept jobs. Similarly, if the higher rate of tax were increased, then people might be less willing to do overtime and more inclined to reduce their working hours, retire early or not seek promotion.

Tax revenues

Some economists consider that, if tax rates are increased too much, tax revenues may actually fall because the disincentives to work are so great. If the higher rate of income tax is increased, then there is likely to be an increase in tax avoidance (legal) and tax evasion (illegal) and a rise in the number of tax exiles. The *Laffer curve* illustrated in Figure 15 shows that, if the marginal tax rate is T then tax revenues will be maximised. However, an increase in the marginal tax rate to V will result in a reduction in tax revenues from R to S.

> **Knowledge check 27**
>
> How would an increase in income tax affect the opportunity cost of work?

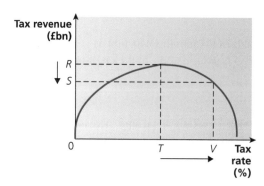

Figure 15 The Laffer curve

Income distribution

Most countries have a *progressive* income tax system so that the proportion of income paid in tax increases as income increases. Consequently, income tax makes income distribution more equitable.

Real output and employment

An increase in income tax rates would cause a fall in disposable income. In turn, this would cause a reduction in consumption and, therefore, a fall in aggregate demand. It may also be argued that the disincentive effects of higher income tax would cause a leftward shift in the aggregate supply curve. Both of these would, therefore, cause a fall in real output and an increase in unemployment.

Figure 16 shows that an increase in income tax rates would cause a fall in disposable income. In turn, this would cause a decrease in consumption and, therefore, in aggregate demand. Consequently, the aggregate demand curve would shift to the left and real output would fall. The disincentive effect of higher income tax rates could cause the aggregate supply curve to shift to the left, so real output would ultimately decrease from Y_1 to Y_2.

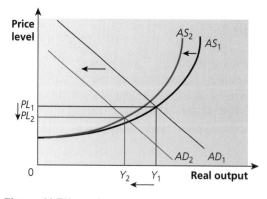

Figure 16 Effect of an increase in income tax rates

The price level

The fall in aggregate demand described above would tend to depress the price level, although this may be offset slightly by a leftward shift in the aggregate supply curve resulting from an increased disincentive to work.

Exam tip

Include an aggregate demand/aggregate supply diagram when considering the implications of changes in income tax.

The trade balance

An increase in income tax rates would cause a fall in disposable income. In turn, this would cause a reduction in consumption and, therefore, a fall in imports. This would result in an improvement in the trade balance.

FDI flows

Higher income tax rates might act as a deterrent to FDI because entrepreneurs and senior managers from the global company would face a decrease in their disposable incomes, assuming they would be based in the country for which the FDI was destined.

The economic effects of changes in indirect tax rates

Incentives to work

Indirect taxes have a less obvious impact on incentives to work than direct taxes. However, it is possible that an increase in indirect taxes will encourage people to work harder so that they can maintain their current standard of living.

Tax revenues

If VAT or other indirect taxes are increased then it is likely that tax revenues will increase. However, there is a danger that placing excessively high taxes on specific products might result in a fall in tax revenues. For example, high taxes on whisky in the UK resulted in less tax revenue, while high taxes on tobacco resulted in a considerable increase in smuggling.

Income distribution

Many indirect taxes have a *regressive effect*, i.e. people on low incomes pay a higher proportion of their incomes in indirect taxes than those on higher incomes. This is particularly true of specific taxes which are a set amount per unit. Consequently, indirect taxes usually make income distribution less equal.

Real output and employment

An increase in indirect tax rates would cause a fall in real income. In turn, this would cause a reduction in consumption and, therefore, a fall in aggregate demand. Consequently, real output and employment would fall.

The price level

The fall in aggregate demand described above would cause a fall in the price level. However, an increase in indirect taxes will raise the price of most goods and services. If workers and trade unions respond by demanding wage increases to compensate for price rises, then an inflationary wage–price spiral could result.

The trade balance

An increase in VAT or excise duties would have no impact on the trade balance. However, an increase in tariffs would reduce imports and so result in an improvement in the trade balance.

Knowledge check 28

How would an increase in income tax rates affect the value of the multiplier?

FDI flows

Higher indirect tax rates might act as a deterrent to FDI because prices of finished products would be higher, so reducing the real income of consumers. However, if the product is primarily aimed at the export market, this may not be a significant consideration.

Other effects of an increase in indirect tax rates

- An increase in indirect tax on a product will cause a leftward shift in the supply curve. The incidence of the tax on consumers and producers depends on the *price elasticity of demand* for the product (see Theme 1).
- The price of the product will increase above marginal cost, so resulting in allocative inefficiency, unless external costs are associated with the production of the product.

Public sector finances

Distinction between automatic stabilisers and discretionary fiscal policy

Fiscal policy refers to the use of government expenditure and taxation in order to influence the level of economic activity in a country. From the 1980s until 2008, its primary role was to ensure stable public finances. However, since 2008 it has once again assumed a role in macroeconomic management not only in the UK but also in China, the USA and a variety of other countries. Key features of fiscal policy include the following:

- *Automatic stabilisers* relate to the fact that some forms of government expenditure and revenues from some taxes change automatically in line with changes in GDP and the state of the economy. These stabilisers help to reduce fluctuations caused by the trade/business cycle. Examples include progressive taxation and welfare payments such as unemployment pay and various means-tested benefits, e.g. pension credits for elderly people living on low incomes.
- *Discretionary fiscal policy* refers to deliberate changes in taxes and public expenditure designed to achieve the government's macroeconomic objectives. For example, the global economic crisis has led many countries to introduce a 'fiscal stimulus' to prevent severe recession. Typically, this has included: increases in public expenditure on infrastructure (roads and bridges in the USA); green technology and targeted subsidies to distressed industries (e.g. the car industry); and tax cuts.

> **Knowledge check 29**
>
> How would public finances be affected by a recession?

Distinction between a fiscal deficit and a national debt

A *fiscal (budget) deficit* occurs when public expenditure (both current and capital) is greater than tax revenues. Public sector net borrowing is the official term used to describe a fiscal deficit. The *national debt* or public sector net debt is the cumulative total of past government borrowing.

Distinction between structural and cyclical deficits

The *'structural' fiscal deficit* is an estimate of how large the deficit would be if the economy were operating at a normal, sustainable level of employment and activity. However, it is difficult to estimate precisely what this 'normal' level would be.

The *'cyclical' fiscal deficit* is that part of the fiscal deficit associated with recession.

Factors influencing the size of fiscal deficits

Factors influencing the size and pattern of public expenditure include the following:

- *GDP*. During a recession, real GDP will be falling. In turn, public expenditure on automatic stabilisers will be rising while tax revenues will be falling. Consequently, fiscal deficits will be increasing. In contrast, during a period of rising real GDP, public expenditure on automatic stabilisers will be falling while tax revenues will be rising and so fiscal deficits will be decreasing. However, the demand for many government-provided services such as health and education rises more than proportionately because demand for them is *income elastic*, putting upward pressure on public expenditure.
- *The size and age distribution of the population*. An increase in the size of the population is likely to mean an increase in public expenditure on health, education and infrastructure. An ageing population will lead to an increase in the dependency ratio, i.e. fewer workers per pensioner. This implies lower tax revenues from workers combined with higher expenditure on pensions to retired people, so causing an increase in fiscal deficits.
- *Discretionary fiscal policy*. The 2008 financial crisis led to the resurrection of fiscal policy as a means of managing the economy in several countries. In July 2015, South Korea pumped $10 billion into its economy to offset falling exports and an outbreak of Middle East respiratory syndrome (MERS).
- *Debt interest*. The massive increase in fiscal deficits from 2008 in the UK and many developed economies led to sharp rises in these countries' national debts (see below). In turn, this is resulting in higher interest payments on the national debt.

Factors influencing the size of national debts

The national debt of a country would be affected by the following:

- *Fiscal deficits or fiscal surpluses*. If a country had persistent fiscal deficits then the national debt would be increasing, whereas if there were persistent surpluses then the size of the national debt is likely to fall.
- *Fiscal deficits might be caused by recessions*, which would result in automatic stabilisers, i.e. government expenditure on means-tested benefits would increase, whereas tax receipts would fall. Further, fiscal deficits might arise because of ageing populations, which result in increased expenditure on state pensions, healthcare and social care.

The significance of the size of fiscal deficits and national debts

Some argue that, if the money is being used to finance improvements in infrastructure and other capital projects, then a large national debt might be justified because it would be increasing a country's future productive potential, so making it easier to repay in the future. However, certain problems may arise:

- There is an *opportunity cost* for future generations. Interest payments on the national debt mean that less money will be available for public services.
- *Crowding out*. If the increasing size of the national debt is an indication of an increase in the size of the public sector, then resource or *financial crowding out* could occur (see page 58).

> **Exam tip**
>
> When answering questions on this area it is useful to have current knowledge of the reasons for recent changes in the size and pattern of public expenditure.

■ *Danger of inflation.* If the rising national debt has been caused by successive fiscal deficits, then there is a danger that inflationary pressures will develop, since injections will be rising relative to leakages.

In the long run, future governments might be forced to raise taxes and/or cut public expenditure so that the national debt can be reduced.

Exam tip

Be sure that you can assess the effects of an increase in the size of the national debt of a country.

Macroeconomic policies in a global context

Use of fiscal policy, monetary policy, exchange rate policy, supply-side policies and direct controls

Measures to reduce fiscal deficits and national debts

To reduce fiscal deficits and national debts a government might increase taxes and/or reduce public expenditure. However, there is a danger that such austerity measures might make the situation worse if the fall in aggregate demand caused by such measures causes a significant fall in real output. The higher unemployment associated with a fall in real output would cause tax revenues to fall, while public expenditure on means-tested benefits would increase.

Measures to reduce poverty and inequality

Governments could take a variety of measures to reduce poverty and inequality, including:
■ increase in means-tested benefits
■ increase in the progressiveness of the tax system, e.g. by increasing the rates of tax on higher incomes and/or by increasing the number of tax rates
■ increase in the national minimum wage
■ subsidised housing for the very poor
■ increased support for children from low-income families, e.g. free childcare for the under-5s; pupil premium, i.e. extra finance to schools based on the number of children from poor backgrounds

Changes in interest rates and the supply of money

Changes in interest rates and the supply of money are part of *monetary policy.*
■ *Interest rate changes.* These are used to influence the cost of money and, in many countries, to achieve the inflation target set by the government. For example, if the inflation rate is predicted to rise above its target, then the Central Bank would increase the base interest rate. However, the use of interest rates has various disadvantages, e.g. the full effect of an increase in the rate of interest takes between 18 and 24 months to work through the economy; business costs rise; the exchange rate of the currency may increase, making a country's goods less price competitive; and if confidence is high, businesses and consumers may continue to borrow and spend.
■ *Changes in the money supply.* In recent years these have been achieved through *quantitative easing.* This relates to the action of the Central Bank in buying up government bonds and corporate bonds from the commercial banks and other financial institutions. This has the effect of increasing bank deposits, thereby giving banks the ability to lend more easily to private and business customers.

Knowledge check 30

What factors might limit the effectiveness of monetary policy?

However, some argue that this policy is unlikely to be effective if the banks are risk averse and remain unwilling to lend unless the loan is risk free. There is also the danger that the increased supply of money in the economy could unleash a serious bout of inflation (based on the monetarist belief in the **quantity theory of money**). An increase in the money supply could also cause a depreciation in the *exchange rate* which, in turn, would result in an increase in net exports and so increase aggregate demand.

Measures to increase international competitiveness

Firms can improve the competitiveness of their products by investing in new capital equipment with the aim of raising productivity. They could improve the design and quality of their products through research and development. Governments can try to improve international competitiveness through a variety of *supply-side policies*. Of particular relevance are the following:

- measures to increase occupational mobility, such as education and training schemes
- macroeconomic stability, e.g. a low and stable inflation rate; sound public finances; a relatively stable exchange rate; steady economic growth
- public sector reform aimed at reducing red tape
- government expenditure to improve infrastructure
- privatisation
- incentives for investment, such as tax breaks if companies use profits for investment rather than for distribution to shareholders

It should be noted that international agreements are likely to prevent individual countries increasing their competitiveness by raising tariffs. For example, the UK cannot simply introduce tariffs on goods from other EU countries because of its legal obligations as a member of the EU. Similarly, most countries are members of the World Trade Organization (WTO), whose rules prevent a country unilaterally imposing protectionist measures unless there is justifiable case.

Further, it is not correct to suggest that 'the UK government could devalue its currency' because the pound is a floating currency. Also, since the Bank of England is independent, the government cannot directly engineer a depreciation in the exchange rate of the pound through a reduction in interest rates because control over interest rates is no longer in its hands.

Use and impact of macroeconomic policies to respond to external shocks to the global economy

Characteristics of external shocks

External shocks to the global economy may take a variety of forms. Examples include:

- a sudden increase in oil prices
- a severe weather event such as a tsunami which has implications for the global economy or a long-lasting drought affecting crops across the world
- a major financial crisis which has repercussions for the global banking system
- wars and civil unrest which disrupt transport links
- cyber-attacks which have implications for communications globally

Quantity theory of money States that there is a direct and proportionate relationship between changes in the money supply and the price level.

Exam tip

Refer back to what you learned in Theme 2 about supply-side policies and look out for new measures being introduced by governments.

Policy responses

The policy response will vary according to the situation and priorities of policymakers. It should be remembered from Theme 1 that economists are unable to conduct laboratory experiments, so policies used at one time in one set of circumstances may have a different impact than exactly the same policy measures used at a different time.

In the 2008 financial crisis, there was a coordinated monetary policy response, which meant that many central banks slashed their base interest rates. In the UK, the base rate was cut to 0.5% in March 2009. In addition, many governments adopted a fiscal stimulus involving cuts in taxes and increases in public expenditure. These measures were designed to prevent a 1930s-style depression.

Measures to control global companies' (transnationals') operations

The regulation of transfer pricing

Global companies may own various subsidiary companies which adopt pricing policies for transactions between these subsidiaries that are aimed at minimising tax liability. They do this by ensuring that the most profit is made in the countries in which corporation tax and other taxes are lowest. In practice, it is very difficult for an individual government to regulate transfer pricing without global agreements.

Limits to government ability to control global companies

Many transnational (global) companies are 'footloose', i.e. they can move easily from one country to another to take advantage of lower operating costs, e.g. wages, corporation tax, labour and environmental regulations. Further, their investment decisions may have a significant impact on the economy of a country. Consequently, it is very difficult for any individual government to control these global companies.

Problems facing policymakers when applying policies

Inaccurate information

Information regarding GDP, the balance of payments on current account and retail sales is notoriously inaccurate and subject to subsequent revisions. This can make it very difficult for policymakers to devise appropriate polices, given that they may be working with data which do not accurately reflect the state of the economy.

Risks and uncertainties

Some commentators consider that the financial crisis has had long-term repercussions for savings and investment. Such uncertainties make it more difficult for policymakers in formulating economic policy.

Similarly, there is considerable uncertainty about the possible long-run impact of quantitative easing in the eurozone. Some monetarist economists argue that it could risk unleashing a massive bout of inflation (because money supply is being increased), while others consider that previous experience in other countries suggests that it will have little effect on the economy.

Exam tip

Supply-side policies may be particularly relevant when considering the topic of international competitiveness.

Inability to control external shocks

Policymakers are usually unable to predict external shocks or their potential consequences. As a result, it may be difficult for them to formulate appropriate policy responses. Such external shocks could include a sudden and dramatic increase in oil and commodity prices; the exit of a country from the eurozone; or political conflict.

Examination skills and concepts

- Ability to apply synoptic concepts when considering the objectives of public expenditure and the use of taxes.
- Ability to distinguish between the different types of tax and their effects.
- Ability to analyse the effects of a change in public expenditure or taxation.
- Ability to understand the difference between a fiscal deficit and a national debt.
- Ability to evaluate the causes and consequences of fiscal imbalances.
- Ability to evaluate the effectiveness of macroeconomic policy instruments (monetary, fiscal and supply-side policies) in the management of the economy.
- Understanding the significance of macroeconomic policy in a global context, especially in the light of major global shocks, e.g. the credit crisis.

Common examination errors

- Weak definitions (e.g. stating that progressive taxes imply that the more you earn, the more you pay. This is imprecise, because it could be true of progressive, proportional and regressive taxes).
- Confusion over the meaning of public expenditure (it is expenditure by the government *not* expenditure by the public, i.e. consumers).
- Confusing a fiscal deficit with a balance of payments deficit on current account.
- Not addressing the question set (e.g. in questions demanding an analysis of an increase in public expenditure, it would be incorrect to focus the answer on the effects of tax increases to fund the extra public expenditure).
- Confusion between the different macroeconomic policy instruments, e.g. between fiscal and supply-side policies.
- Omission of *AD/AS* diagrams and analysis in discussing macroeconomic issues.
- Failure to consider the broader effects of the use of macroeconomic policies, e.g. the impact of interest rate changes on the exchange rate.
- Failure to explain the transmission mechanisms fully.

Content Guidance

Links and common themes

There is plenty of opportunity to include concepts covered in previous themes in this section. In particular, Theme 4 builds on the material covered in Theme 2, so it is worth reviewing that carefully. The following are some examples:

■ Discussion of *price elasticity of demand* (Theme 1) when considering the impact of an increase in indirect taxes or subsidies.
■ Consideration of *opportunity cost* (Theme 1) when discussing public expenditure.
■ Link with demand-side and supply-side policies (Theme 2).

Summary

■ The public sector plays a significant role in the macroeconomy in many developed economies. For example, in the UK, public expenditure was nearly 45% of GDP in 2014/15.
■ There are three different forms of public expenditure: capital (on long-term projects such as roads), current (day-to-day expenditure) and transfer payments (expenditure for which there is no production in return).
■ There are three different categories of taxes: progressive, proportional and regressive; and two distinct types: direct (on income and wealth) and indirect (on expenditure).

■ The relationship between public expenditure and tax revenues is expressed in terms of a fiscal surplus or fiscal deficit.
■ Fiscal policy involves the use of changes in public expenditure and taxation to influence the level of economic activity.
■ Monetary policy involves the use of changes in interest rates and money supply to influence the level of economic activity.
■ Supply-side policies are designed to influence the supply side of the economy through increasing competition and incentives aimed at increasing productivity.

Questions & Answers

Exam format

Theme 4 will be tested in both Paper 2 and Paper 3 of the examination. You will find that Theme 4 builds on Theme 2. It repeats ideas but goes more deeply into the detail and wider implications (global rather than just UK). You should therefore use your Theme 2 and Theme 4 books together in your preparation for Paper 2 to gain a firm understanding of macroeconomics.

Paper 2 comprises 35% of the weighting for the A-level examination. The time allowed is 2 hours. Paper 2 of the A-level specification will include some Theme 2 concepts and some Theme 4 concepts. There are three sections, with Section A worth 25 marks, Section B worth 50 marks and Section C (the essay section) worth 25 marks — total 100 marks. You will have choice in Section C, and this will be a choice from two macroeconomic essays.

Paper 3 of the A-level is synoptic and covers content from all four themes. It is worth 30% of the total qualification and the time allowed is 2 hours. The paper consists of two sections, with each section containing one data-response question broken down into four parts. The last part of each of these data-response questions provides a choice of extended open-response essay questions and you will have to select one question from a choice of two. The total mark for the paper is 100 marks, with each section worth 50 marks. Questions in both sections will require understanding of both microeconomics and macroeconomics. You will need to make connections with the content of this guide with that of the other themes. Therefore, you should use all four Student Guides to prepare for this paper.

The questions that follow should be used for practice for the A-level examination only, because the material goes beyond that required for AS. Note that they have not been accredited for Edexcel and the author has no knowledge of future examination papers, apart from the sample assessment materials (SAMs) which are available freely online. The questions focus mainly on the content covered in Theme 4 but will be useful as a practice after studying the second year of the A-level course.

There is a 'levels'-based approach to marking most of the data-response questions and open extended questions. This enables a variety of different approaches in student answers to be valid rather than solely requiring specific points that are stated on the mark scheme. It means the examiner makes an initial assessment of the quality of an answer and places it at a level ranging from 1 to 4. The examiner's judgement is then refined to award a more precise mark within that level. It is recommended that you refer to the levels descriptors provided at the end of the longer questions in the sample assessment materials for Economics on the Edexcel website:
www.edexcel.com/quals/gce/gce15/economics/Pages/default.aspx

In addition, the levels-based mark scheme is often broken down into two further parts: the first focuses on 'knowledge, application and analysis' marks and the second relates to 'evaluation'. The command words used for evaluation questions are: *examine, evaluate, assess, discuss* and *to what extent*. Any of these words in the question indicate that you should demonstrate some critical understanding of the issues being discussed.

For **A-level Paper 2**, the following are the only command words that will be used:

Section A Short-answer questions — *Define, Calculate, Explain*

Section B

- *Examine* (8 marks) x 1
- *Assess* (10 marks) x 1
- *Discuss* (12 or 15 marks) x 2

Section C

- *Evaluate/To what extent* (25 marks) — choose one from two

For **A-level Paper 3**, the following are the only command words that will be used:

Sections A and B

- *Explain* (5 marks)
- *Examine* (8 marks)
- *Discuss* (12 marks)
- *Evaluate/To what extent* (25 marks) — choose one from two

Assessment objectives

There are four assessment objectives (AOs) in each theme of A-level economics, namely *knowledge, application, analysis* and *evaluation*. Across the three A-level papers the weighting ranges are as follows:

Objective	Assessment objectives	Weighting
1	Knowledge and understanding: demonstrate knowledge and understanding of the specified content	22–24%
2	Application: apply knowledge and understanding of the specified content to problems and issues arising from both familiar and unfamiliar situations	22–24%
3	Analysis: analyse economic problems and issues	26–28%
4	Evaluation: evaluate economic arguments and evidence, making informed judgements	26–28%

The command words used in the questions should give a clear indication as to which skills are being tested. It is essential that you understand the meaning behind these words, so that you are sure about what is being expected. Some of the key command words are defined on pages 72–73.

Knowledge and understanding

This objective involves the ability to define key words and terms, together with an ability to understand the economic theories and models that you are expected to use in the examination. In Theme 4, you should be able to define terms that you have learned from previous themes, as well as concepts such as globalisation, international competitiveness, balance of payment deficit/surplus on current account, poverty, fiscal surplus/deficit and economic development.

Application

This assessment objective may be demonstrated by an ability to apply knowledge and understanding to particular contexts. It is likely that essays and, more especially, data-response questions will be set in a real-world context, so generalised responses are unlikely to score highly.

Analysis

Analysis is a multi-stage process and therefore involves developing a logical line of argument in a series of steps. This skill (along with evaluation) is particularly important in answering questions on this theme, so practice is essential. Typically, analysis is likely to involve drawing a diagram (such as an aggregate-demand/aggregate-supply diagram) and then explaining the changes that have occurred. For example, a question might require analysis of how a recession in the USA might impact on other countries; how a significant change in commodity prices affects the global economy; or how a dramatic appreciation of one country's currency might affect that country's economy and those of its major trading partners.

Evaluation

This objective requires you to demonstrate a critical approach to the subject/data under consideration. This is a challenging task but since evaluation carries 26–28% of the total marks, it is vital to ensure that this skill is demonstrated where required. The first issue is to detect when evaluation is required. The command word is the key. Any question using any of the following command words implies that evaluation must be included: *examine*; *assess*; *evaluate*; *to what extent*; *discuss*. In practice, most of the data-response questions and the open-ended essay questions require evaluation. The second issue is to devise strategies for evaluation, which could include the following:

- short- and long-run effects
- the magnitude of an effect
- questioning the validity of the assumptions behind a theory or model
- the reliability and validity of the data
- missing information
- advantages and disadvantages of an argument
- differential effects on different stakeholders
- prioritising the effects in terms of the most/least significant

Grade boundaries

Obviously you will be aiming high, so the performance descriptors for the A/B boundary as formulated by all the examination boards are given below. Further comments *in italics* are made by the author of this guide.

Knowledge

Candidates characteristically demonstrate:

- detailed knowledge of a range of facts and concepts
- clear understanding of terminology, institutions and models
- detailed knowledge and clear understanding of the interconnections between the different elements of the subject content

Essentially you must be able to include precise definitions in your answers, identify key points relevant to the question and know relevant information about the global economy.

Application

Candidates characteristically apply concepts, numerical and graphical techniques and terminology to complex issues arising in familiar and unfamiliar situations.

You must be able to support your essay answers by including relevant examples and make effective use of the information provided in the data questions. This may involve calculations and illustrating your answer with diagrams.

Analysis

Candidates characteristically:

- select relevant concepts, models, theories and techniques
- demonstrate, for the most part, development of logical explanations for complex economic problems and issues, with focus and relevance

This skill involves using the economist's toolbox of concepts, models and theories and explaining the steps of an argument in a logical way. Remember that analysis is a multi-stage process requiring a detailed breakdown of how, for example, a change in the availability of credit will work through the economy.

Evaluation

Candidates characteristically:

- evaluate complex economic arguments
- prioritise evidence and arguments
- make reasoned arguments
- reach and present supported conclusions
- make reasoned recommendations

Typically, a good piece of evaluation will involve a critical approach to the question which demonstrates that rarely in economics will there be an unequivocal answer to a question.

Key command words

Define You should give a clear and precise meaning of a term or concept.

Explain You should give reasons for a particular situation or changes in a variable.

Analyse This requires you to give a multi-stage process of explanation including identification of assumptions; relevant diagrams; and a step-by-step account of, for example, how a change in a variable might impact on different economic agents.

Evaluate, **examine**, **assess**, **discuss** and **to what extent** All these are evaluative command words that require you to offer critical appraisal of a situation or of the potential effects of a change in a variable. Evaluation may be demonstrated by examination of issues such as the magnitude of the change; the time frame under which the effects will occur (i.e. short-run and long-run effects); the advantages and disadvantages of the change; the relative importance of the factors identified; consideration of the reliability and validity of the data provided; identification of missing information which might make a judgement difficult; and the realism of the assumptions made.

How to answer short-answer questions

This advice relates to the Section A questions in Paper 2.

- Each of the five questions is worth 5 marks.
- One part of each question will be a multiple-choice question worth 1 mark.
- The other part will be worth 4 marks or there will be two parts, each worth 2 marks.
- Calculations may be required. If this is the case, then show your workings because marks may be awarded for the correct method even if the answer is incorrect. Also remember to include the relevant units associated with the numbers.

How to answer data-response questions

All data used for these questions are drawn from published sources, so frequent reading of articles related to economics will pay considerable dividends. Among the most common sources for questions used in examination papers are the the *Financial Times*, *The Times*, *The Independent*, *The Guardian* and the *Daily Telegraph* as well as sources of official data such as ONS, Eurostat, OECD, IMF and the World Bank.

Here are some further tips for answering data-response questions:

- **Check graphs and data.** To avoid making mistakes in interpretation of graphs and data, it is important to:
  - check the axis titles
  - look at the scale of the charts
  - identify possible trends. In this context it may be useful to calculate percentage changes because these are often more meaningful than absolute changes.
  - consider whether the data are sufficient or whether other information would be helpful
  - question the validity or reliability of the data. Remember that selective use of data can give a very misleading picture.
- **Show your calculations.** Some short-answer and multiple-choice questions may require calculations. It is important to show your workings because marks may be awarded for the correct method even if the answer is incorrect.
- **Remember to include units.** In answering calculation questions, include the relevant unit in your answer, where appropriate. For example, the answer might be 10 billion euros so the answer should be written €10bn not just 10!

- **Check the command words.** Not all the data questions will require evaluation, so be sure to look out for those that do.
- **Define key terms.** Remember that 20% of the marks available for these questions are awarded for knowledge, so do not forget to define a key term which appears in the question or one which is pertinent in your answer.
- **Make use of the information provided.** There is a danger of writing generalised answers to the questions. To avoid this, ensure that appropriate use is made of the information provided because this could enable you to gain marks for application to the context. For example, it might be possible to do some simple calculations to demonstrate the changes in the size of a budget deficit.
- **Apply economic concepts and theories.** It should be possible to apply a wide range of concepts in your answers. Appropriate use should be made of the *AD/AS* model and, in addition, concepts from previous themes.
- **Include diagrammatic analysis.** Some questions might specifically require a diagram to be drawn, such as one illustrating the effects of a tariff. However, even where one is not specifically requested, there may be opportunities to include diagrams. These can be an invaluable part of your analysis, not least because they can reduce the amount that you need to write. Nevertheless, it is important to integrate diagrams fully into your written analysis — do not just include a diagram without any reference to it in your response.
- **Plan your time carefully.** As a rough guide, the number of marks indicates the number of minutes that you should spend on each part. This allows some time for reading the associated information and checking your answer at the end. A common mistake is for students to spend far too long answering questions which are worth relatively few marks, leaving themselves insufficient time to answer the questions with larger mark bases. In particular, avoid spending too much time on the data-response questions, otherwise you will leave yourself insufficient time to answer the essay questions fully.
- **Practise.** Completing the questions under timed conditions presents various challenges, not least the danger of spending too much time on the initial questions at the expense of the later questions which carry higher marks. Practising the questions included in this book or those from past examination papers will provide invaluable experience and enable you to enhance your skills.

How to answer extended open-response (essay) questions

In both Paper 2 and Paper 3 there are 25-mark questions which have to be answered. In both these papers there is a choice of questions. Here are some guidelines for tackling these questions:

- **Select your question carefully.** In particular, ensure that you are able to answer the question fully and that you are able to apply relevant economic analysis.
- **Plan your answer.** Write down key words or phrases that will form the basis of the paragraphs or draw a mind map indicating the areas that you intend to cover. This approach might enable you to think more broadly: all too often essay answers are focused too narrowly. Remember that you should aim to write an answer which

demonstrates both depth and breadth. In the Paper 3 essay, you will be expected to include elements of both microeconomics and macroeconomics.

■ **Define key concepts and terms in the question.** It will quickly become apparent to an examiner if you are uncertain about a concept, so it is better to explain the concepts and terms precisely in your introductory paragraph.

■ **Apply economic concepts and theories wherever possible.** Remember that Paper 3 is a synoptic paper, so you need to demonstrate your facility with concepts learned from different parts of the specification, both micro and macro.

■ **Practise your analytical writing skills.** Remember that analysis is a multi-stage process, so practise the skill of developing logical and carefully reasoned answers. For example, consider the implications of the withdrawal of foreign direct investment on a country's economy.

■ **Include diagrammatic analysis.** This theme provides considerable scope for including aggregate-demand/aggregate-supply analysis, especially in the context of international economics; the application of monetary, fiscal and supply-side policies; and foreign direct investment. However, there is also the opportunity of using production possibility frontiers, e.g. in the context of comparative advantage, as well as microeconomic supply and demand diagrams (perhaps in the context of tariffs or to illustrate the causes of changes in commodity prices in the context of developing countries).

■ **Use your knowledge about current economic issues.** Both the essays and data-response questions usually provide an opportunity to demonstrate your knowledge about current issues. Generalised answers and those based solely on a theoretical approach are unlikely to secure the highest marks.

■ **Allocate your time carefully.** You should allow yourself at least 30 minutes for writing the answer to a 25-mark essay question. This ensures you have time for planning your answer and for checking your response at the end.

■ **Evaluate.** It is a good idea to evaluate the issues discussed in each paragraph. It is also useful to include an evaluative conclusion at the end of your answer to each part of the question.

■ **Practise.** Writing an essay under timed conditions is a challenge. It is easy to lose focus, spend too much time on the first part of the essay or not write in a structured, logical manner. Effort spent practising writing essays can, therefore, really enhance your examination performance. It is a good idea to start by writing an answer to a question that you have already planned and then go on to tackle unfamiliar questions.

The A* grade

To secure an A* grade it is necessary to demonstrate depth and breadth in your knowledge, understanding, analytical and evaluative skills. These skills are required especially in answering the extended open-response questions. Further, it is necessary to demonstrate a facility with the quantitative skills relevant to economics.

The standard required is challenging and typically you would need a score of around 80% of the raw marks. On the basis of the previous specifications, only a small proportion of students are expected to be awarded A* grades.

Paper 2

Section A

Question 1 Law of comparative advantage

The figure below shows production possibility frontiers for two countries, A and B.

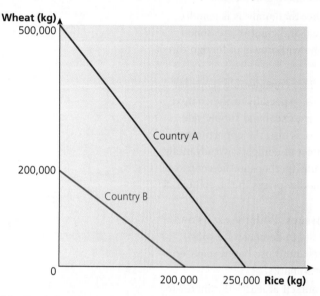

(a) Explain whether country A should specialise in wheat or rice. (4 marks)

(b) According to the law of comparative advantage, if each country specialises and trades in the product in which it has a comparative advantage, then: (1 mark)

A output will increase

B exports and imports will fall

C consumer welfare will fall

D absolute poverty will increase

Student answer

(a) To determine which country should specialise in each product it is necessary to calculate and then compare the opportunity cost ratios.

	Opportunity cost of producing 1 kg of wheat	Opportunity cost of producing 1 kg of rice
A	½	2
B	1	1

With regard to wheat, country A has a lower opportunity cost than country B whereas with regard to rice, country B has a lower opportunity cost than country A. Therefore, country A should specialise in wheat and country B should specialise in rice.

ℯ 4/4 marks awarded. The answer includes calculation of opportunity cost ratios, which is a very good way of approaching the question because this enables the comparative advantage of each country to be determined easily. The accompanying explanation provides sound analysis and this answer, therefore, scores maximum marks.

(b) A

ℯ 1/1 mark awarded. This is the correct answer because, according to the law of comparative advantage, specialisation and trade will lead to increased output.

Question 2 Exchange rates

The exchange rate of the pound sterling changed from €1.04 in January 2009 to €1.43 in July 2015.

(a) Calculate the percentage change in the value of the £ against the €. (2 marks)

(b) Explain the effect of this change in the value of the pound on the competitiveness of UK goods in the eurozone. (2 marks)

(c) The exchange rate of a country's currency is likely to appreciate against other currencies if: (1 mark)

    A there is an increase in the country's current account deficit

    B there is a decrease in foreign direct investment into the country

    C the state of the economy is expected to deteriorate

    D the country's central bank raises the base interest rate

Student answer

(a) $\frac{39}{104} \times 100 = 37.5\%$

In other words, the value of the pound appreciated considerably against the euro during this period.

ℯ 2/2 marks awarded. The answer shows the steps in the calculation, which is important because if a mistake is made in the calculation itself, marks may still be gained for the method used. In this case the calculation is correct and is supported by a correct interpretation of the result.

(b) This will decrease the competitiveness of the UK's goods and services in the eurozone.

ℯ 1/2 marks awarded. The answer given is correct but it could be supported with a bit more reasoning. For example, it could be stated that the foreign currency price of exports would be higher while the domestic price of imported goods would be lower.

(c) D

ⓔ **1/1 mark awarded.** Answer D is the correct answer because higher interest rates will make it more attractive for foreigners to place money in the country's banks, so increasing the demand for sterling on the foreign exchange market.

Question 3 Financial sector

(a) A key function of a central bank is: (1 mark)

    A to implement the government's fiscal policy

    B to raise money for companies

    C to act as banker to the banks

    D to take deposits from members of the public

(b) Explain two possible market failures in the financial sector. (4 marks)

> **Student answer**
>
> **(a)** C

ⓔ **1/1 mark awarded.** Answer C is correct because central banks hold the accounts of the other banks in their country.

> **(b)** If banks are bailed out by the government when they are in danger of going bust, then there is a 'moral hazard'. In other words, there is the prospect that banks would again act irresponsibly in the future because they know that the government would always rescue them if they were in difficulties.

ⓔ **2/4 marks awarded.** One market failure is explained well. However, to score full marks it is necessary to consider another market failure associated with banking: for example, asymmetric information.

Question 4 Inequality

In the diagram there are two Lorenz curves representing two countries, Denmark and Namibia.

(a) What might be inferred from the chart? (1 mark)

    A Indirect taxes must be higher in Denmark than in Namibia.

    B Income distribution is more even in Denmark than in Namibia.

    C Income tax rates are higher in Namibia than in Denmark.

    D GDP per capita is higher in Namibia than in Denmark.

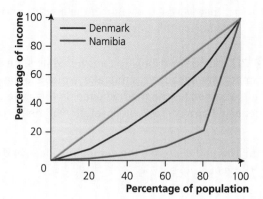

(b) With reference to the chart, explain how inequality is measured. (2 marks)

(c) Explain one reason for the difference in income inequality in Namibia and Denmark. (2 marks)

Student answer

(a) B

🅔 **1/1 mark awarded.** It is correctly stated that B is the answer. This is because the Lorenz curve for Denmark is closer to the 45° line than that for Namibia.

(b) Income inequality is measured using the Gini coefficient.

🅔 **1/2 marks awarded.** The mention of the Gini coefficient is worth 1 mark. However, to score full marks it would be necessary to explain exactly how it is calculated.

(c) Denmark is a more developed economy than Namibia with a higher GDP per capita. Consequently, it is able to adopt policies to redistribute incomes from the rich to the poor. For example, the government could give means-tested benefits to the poor and use progressive taxation to redistribute income from those on high incomes to those on low incomes.

🅔 **2/2 marks awarded.** This provides a comprehensive response to the question and scores full marks.

Question 5 Balance of payments

The chart below shows German imports and exports between 1999 and 2014.

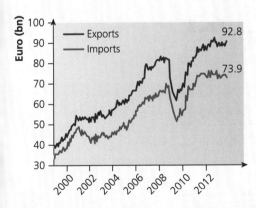

(a) Which of the following can be inferred from the chart?   (1 mark)

   A   The trade balance would cause aggregate demand to increase.

   B   There is a budget surplus throughout the period.

   C   The trade balance was always negative.

   D   Withdrawals are greater than injections.

(b) Explain the likely effect of a decrease in German income tax rates on the German trade balance.   (4 marks)

Student answer

(a) A

ⓔ 1/1 mark awarded. A is the correct answer because the chart shows that, in every year, the value of exports (an injection) was greater than the value of imports (a leakage).

(b) If there is a decrease in income tax rates then the disposable income of workers will increase. In turn, this will lead to an increase in consumer expenditure. As a result, there will be an increase in imports because some of the extra consumption will be spent on imported goods.

ⓔ 3/4 marks awarded. This answer provides a clear chain of reasoning as far as it goes. However, the last link is missing, i.e. there should be a concluding sentence explaining that higher imports would lead to a reduction in the balance of trade surplus.

Section B

Question 6 The Greek economy

Economic indicators for Greece

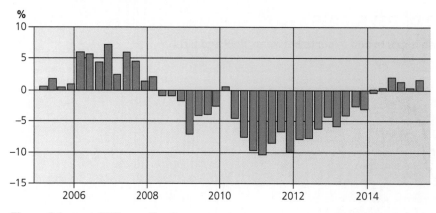

Figure 1 Annual GDP growth rate

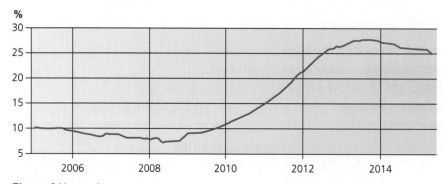

Figure 2 Unemployment rate

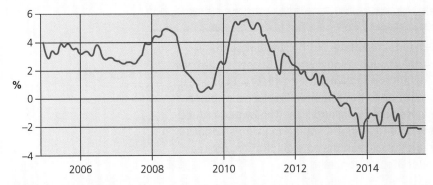

Figure 3 CPI inflation rate

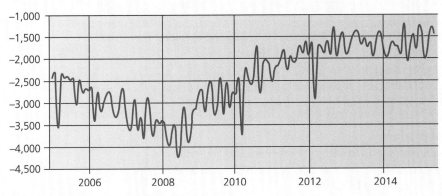

Figure 4 Balance of trade (€ millions)

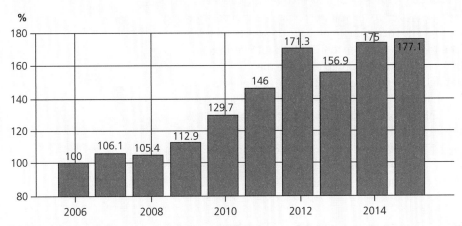

Figure 5 National debt as a proportion of GDP

Source: All data from Trading Economics website, www.tradingeconomics.com/greece

Extract 1 The third Greek bailout

In 2015, the Greek government had to negotiate another bailout so that it could repay debts to the IMF. Without such an agreement, Greece would have had to leave the eurozone and default on repayment of its debts. Economists have estimated that if Greece returned to the drachma (its currency before it joined the euro) then it would depreciate by around 50%. This would reduce the country's terms of trade and lead to a significant fall in living standards. A particular problem would be a sharp rise in the rate of inflation, not least because most food and raw materials are imported.

The terms of the bailout were very stringent and include the following:
- Further cuts in public expenditure on social services and pensions and the end of fuel tax benefits for farmers
- An increase in the top rate of VAT from 13% to 23% on some goods and services including restaurants and removal of discounts on VAT on Greek islands
- A rise in the statutory retirement age to 67 by 2022
- Reinstate key reforms in the healthcare system, including: scrapping price controls for medicines; increasing centralised procurement of hospital supplies
- Deregulate the natural gas market
- Relaunch privatisation, including plans to sell port facilities and regional airports with the aim of raising €50bn, much of which would be used to recapitalise the banks and to repay debts

Several economists have argued that these further austerity measures are doomed to failure. Keynes argued in his masterpiece *The Economic Consequences of the Peace* that squeezing a ruined country was in no one's best interests (as was done to Germany after the First World War in the Versailles Treaty). The IMF has been unwilling to approve the deal because it thinks that some form of debt relief and restructuring is essential. Such views are unsurprising given that Greece's GDP has fallen by 25% since 2008, unemployment is around 26% and youth unemployment is over 50%. More worryingly, Greece is experiencing significant emigration of workers, especially of those with high skills. Without a period of significant and sustained growth, the debt to GDP ratio is certain to increase: some have predicted that this will reach over 200% in the near future.

(a) With reference to Figures 1, 2 and 3, how might the relationship between unemployment and the rate of inflation between 2010 and 2014 be explained? (5 marks)

ⓔ This question demands clear references to the data followed by an explanation for the relationship described.

(b) With reference to the information provided, examine the performance of the Greek economy since 2008. (8 marks)

ⓔ The key word here is 'examine', which is an evaluative command word. Once again, reference should be made to the information provided: a generic response will not earn full credit.

(c) Assess two possible implications of Greece being forced to leave the eurozone. (10 marks)

ⓔ Again, evaluation is required because the command word is 'assess'. It is also important to discuss just two implications.

(d) Discuss the case for the Greek government taking measures to reduce its national debt as quickly as possible. (12 marks)

ⓔ This question asks you to consider the disadvantages of running a large national debt for Greece (or, indeed, other countries). With a 12-mark question it is best to confine your answer to an examination of about three issues so that there is time for sufficient analysis and evaluation.

(e) With reference to the information provided, discuss the likely economic effects of the bailout conditions designed to reduce Greece's national debt. (15 marks)

ⓔ This is a fairly open-ended question so it is necessary to select a few measures so that these may be examined fully — rather that considering many measures but only analysing their effects superficially. It is also necessary to consider the overall effect of these measures on the Greek economy. As with the other questions in Section B, except part (a), evaluation is required.

Student answer

(a) During much of the period between 2011 and 2014 there were significant falls in Greece's GDP. Inevitably, this resulted in an increase in the unemployment rate from about 11% to 27%. Meanwhile, the rate of inflation fell from 3% at the start of 2010 to –3% in 2014. This inverse relationship may be explained by reference to the Phillips curve as shown below:

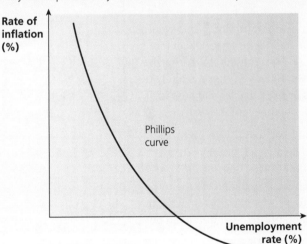

The inverse relationship may be explained as follows: with negative growth rates, and increasing unemployment, there is a decrease in aggregate demand so reducing wage inflationary pressures. Therefore, the very significant increase in unemployment in Greece (associated with recession) would cause a decrease in the rate of inflation.

Questions & Answers

5/5 marks awarded. This answer starts by making good use of the data and then analyses it by reference to the Phillips curve followed by a clear explanation.

(b) The data show that, since 2008, there has been a significant fall in GDP with negative growth rates in most quarters until 2014. This is reflected in the unemployment data, which show an increase from around 7% in 2008 to over 25% in 2014.

The weak state of the Greek economy is also illustrated in the inflation data: from just after the beginning of 2010 the inflation rate has fallen from just below 6% to deflation from 2013. This might indicate weak aggregate demand in the economy.

The national debt to GDP ratio has risen significantly from 100% in 2006 to 177% in 2015. This reflects both the fiscal deficits and negative growth rates in many years since 2008, once again indicating the poor state of the economy since 2008.

Despite the poor performance of the Greek economy since 2008, there are some positive signs: the positive growth rates in GDP since 2014; the slight decrease in unemployment and the decrease in the trade deficit since 2008.

ⓔ **8/8 marks awarded.** The first three paragraphs make good use of the data and draw appropriate conclusions. The final paragraph is evaluative because it suggests that there are signs of improvement in the Greek economy.

(c) If Greece were forced out of the eurozone it would have to reintroduce its own currency, the drachma. Given the weakness of the Greek economy, it is very likely that its currency would depreciate substantially. **a** This would increase the competitiveness of the Greek goods and services: exports would be cheaper and imports more expensive. This could help to improve the current account of the balance of payments. However, there is likely to be a time lag because traders have contracts at fixed prices and stocks of imported goods mean that price rises will not be apparent immediately. **b**

Greece has to import many raw materials and food so if there is a large depreciation of the drachma, there is likely to be a rapid increase in the rate of inflation, which would reduce real incomes. This increase in cost–push inflation would cause the aggregate supply curve to shift to the left, which would result in a fall in real output. In turn, this is likely to cause an increase in unemployment. However, the rate of inflation is influenced by other factors such as global changes in commodity prices. For example, if commodity prices are falling then this would reduce inflationary pressures in Greece. **c**

ⓔ **8/10 marks awarded.** ⓐ This is a good start to the answer but there could be further explanation of why there is likely to be such a significant fall in the value of the drachma, e.g. loss of confidence by foreign investors or domestic citizens taking their money out of Greece. ⓑ A relevant discussion of the impact on competitiveness includes some evaluation at the end. To develop this further, reference could be made to the Marshall–Lerner condition. ⓒ The answer ends with a good paragraph on the possible inflationary consequences of the depreciation of the currency. To improve further, the analysis could be illustrated with an aggregate supply/aggregate demand diagram.

(d) National debt is the cumulative total of past government borrowing. Large national debts occur when governments have persistent fiscal deficits. The government has to finance the national debt by issuing government bonds. ⓐ An increasing national debt would imply that more bonds must be issued which would drive down their price and increase their yield (interest rate). This increase in interest rates may lead to the crowding out of private sector investment because businesses would face an increase in the rate of interest on loans. It is argued that the private sector allocates resources more efficiently than the state due to the profit motive so there may be a welfare loss to society because the private sector firms are deterred from borrowing by the higher cost involved. ⓑ

Over the last few years Greece's national debt has been increasing as a proportion of GDP and it is predicted to exceed 200% of GDP. This means that debt interest payments will continue to increase which means there is an opportunity cost in terms of expenditure on, for example, health and education. However, if the increase in the national debt is being caused by increased investment by the Greek government on, for example, infrastructure then this may bring benefits to the Greek economy in the longer term. ⓒ

In addition, this high and increasing debt to GDP ratio could lead to a reduction in the country's credit rating which could result in a further increase in interest rates on loans. However, if investors think that the ECB would be willing to continue to bail out Greece then the impact on interest rates on loans may be insignificant. ⓓ

The increase of the national debt to over 200% of Greece's GDP raises the prospect that the government will default on its debt which may further reduce confidence in its economy. However, some economists suggest that it is already impossible for Greece to repay its debts and that some restructuring or default is inevitable. ⓔ

ⓔ 8/12 marks awarded. ⓐ It is always good practice to begin the answer with a clear definition of the key term(s), as is done here. **ⓑ** The crowding out argument is explained well, although there could be some evaluation of it, e.g. by considering the magnitude of the interest rate increase. **ⓒ** This paragraph has considered another relevant issue: namely, the implications of the cost of debt servicing, together with relevant evaluation. **ⓓ** This is a brief point on Greece's credit rating, which is valid but could be developed more fully. **ⓔ** Another brief but relevant point is made. Given the nature of the question, it might be advisable to include a concluding paragraph which makes informed judgements based on the arguments presented.

(e) One measure is to increase the top rate of VAT to a wider range of products and services including restaurants. In theory, this should increase tax revenues because VAT is difficult to avoid and also because people might want to work longer hours in order to maintain their standard of living. However, these higher taxes could cause aggregate demand to fall, which might result in higher unemployment and slower economic growth. In turn, this could mean that the fiscal deficit increases as expenditure on benefits increases and tax revenues fall. **ⓐ**

The increased VAT on restaurants and the removal of VAT tax concessions on Greek islands might have an adverse effect on the tourist industry, which is an important source of foreign currency earnings. In turn, this could cause a deterioration in the current account of the balance of payments. However, many tourists may not be deterred by these measures because Greece is regarded as being cheap relative to some other countries in the eurozone. **ⓑ**

A measure to raise money is the privatisation programme including the ports, airports and infrastructure. It is hoped that this will raise €50 billion and that this will be placed in a special fund to be used primarily to recapitalise the banks and repay debts. Privatisation is designed not only to raise revenue but also to increase efficiency resulting from competition and the profit motive. However, it is uncertain that the assets to be sold will generate €50bn. Further, there is a danger that privatisation will result in the creation of privately owned monopolies which exploit consumers by charging high prices. **ⓒ**

Overall, these measures are designed to increase tax revenues and reduce public expenditure so that Greece runs a budget surplus enabling the national debt to be reduced. However, these measures would reduce aggregate demand and so could cause a further decline in GDP, which would cause national debt as a proportion of GDP to increase. **ⓓ**

ⓔ 12/15 marks awarded. ⓐ The opening paragraph examines the effect of VAT on tax revenues and makes relevant points relating to why this may or may not be the case. **ⓑ** Similarly, the next paragraph considers the possible negative impact on the tourist industry with some relevant evaluation of this point. **ⓒ** This paragraph considers the possible impact of privatisation on the Greek economy and includes some pertinent evaluation. **ⓓ** The final paragraph considers the overall impact of the bailout measures and contains relevant points. However, this should be developed further to include more detailed analysis of their possible impact on the Greek economy and on the whole euro project.

Section C

Question 7 Deflation

Several countries are expected to experience deflation in 2015 including Greece, Bulgaria, Croatia, Poland, Spain and Sweden.

Evaluate the possible benefits of a sustained period of deflation.   (25 marks)

ⓔ The command word indicates that evaluation is essential in answering this question. Its significance is illustrated by the mark allocation for this skill: 9 marks. The marks for the other assessment objectives are: knowledge 4; application 4; and analysis 8. Therefore, the essay places great emphasis on analysis and evaluation.

Student answer

Deflation refers to a fall in the general price level. **ⓐ** The consequences of deflation depend, to a large extent, on the causes. Broadly, there are two types of deflation: 'good' deflation and 'bad' deflation. The potential benefits of deflation mainly arise from 'good' deflation, which is usually associated with improvements in technology which results in improvements in productivity. These result in a rightward shift in the long-run aggregate supply curve. As shown in the diagram below, this causes a rise in real output and a fall in the price level. **ⓑ**

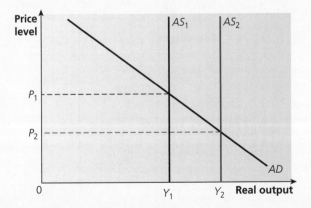

Such good deflation may be beneficial for several reasons. First, a fall in the average price level might result in an increase in the international competitiveness of UK goods and services. This would cause an increase in demand for UK exports and a fall in demand for imports, so improving the trade balance. However, if these improvements in technology are global in nature then the benefits are likely to be spread across all countries, so no single country will gain a competitive advantage.

Second, consumers benefit from rising real incomes, assuming their incomes are constant or rising and the average level of prices is falling. Lower prices imply an increase in consumer surplus (the difference between consumers' willingness to pay and the market price). Further, assuming that incomes are constant or rising, consumers will benefit from higher living standards because they will be able to afford more goods and services. However, consumers with mortgages or debts, e.g. money borrowed on credit cards, will face the problem that the real value of their debts will be rising. c

For businesses, 'good' deflation implies lower costs of production, which could enable them to make higher profits which, in turn, might encourage them to increase investment in, for example, new capital equipment. However, lower prices might result in lower revenues for firms and so there may be no extra finance available for investment. d

However, deflation might result in some disadvantages. In particular, 'bad' deflation is associated with falling aggregate demand, which might be the result of a recession caused by a decrease in consumption, investment, government expenditure and exports. The following diagram illustrates the impact of a decrease in aggregate demand on real output and the price level. e

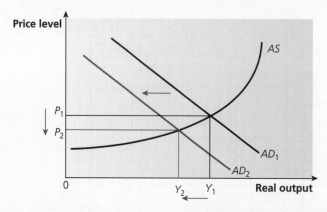

The decrease in aggregate demand causes a leftward shift in the *AD* curve, so causing a fall in real output and a fall in the price level. For the economy this would imply lower living standards since the reduction in real output would result in higher unemployment. There is also the likelihood that income inequality would increase as a direct result of rising unemployment. This type of inflation might result in consumers deferring expenditure in the expectation that prices will fall further. Similarly, firms might defer investment expenditure because of falling demand and falling profits. Falling consumption and investment would cause a further fall in aggregate demand, which could result in a 1930s-style depression. f

For consumers and workers 'bad' deflation might be associated with higher unemployment because firms face falling demand for their goods and services. Further, workers might suffer a decrease in wages as firms try to reduce costs at a time when prices are falling. However, if nominal wages remain constant, consumers would enjoy an increase in their real incomes. g

With demand for goods and services decreasing, the revenues and profits of firms are likely to be falling. Indeed, some would be forced out of business altogether if they are unable to reduce their costs. However, if this deflation only affects one country then its goods and services would become more internationally competitive, which should result in an improvement in its balance of trade. h

As with 'good' deflation, 'bad' deflation also increases the real value of debts for consumers, businesses and the government. In the case of the government, this arises because the real value of the national debt will be increasing at a time when the means of servicing it would be increasing. This indicates serious disadvantages associated with deflation, although consumers and businesses with savings would find that their real value would be increasing. i

It can be seen that there may be many positive outcomes resulting from 'good' deflation because it is associated with higher productivity and higher living standards. In contrast, there are serious dangers associated with falling prices resulting from decreasing aggregate demand, not least that it could result in a prolonged depression. Both types of deflation would be undesirable, however, if the period of falling prices lasted a long time. In conclusion, therefore, much depends on the causes of the deflation and how long it lasts. j

e **23/25 marks awarded.** a The student starts with an accurate definition. b There is a clear reference to the benefits of 'good' deflation to the economy, illustrated with an accurate *AD/AS* diagram. c This is an effective paragraph which explains the benefits of good deflation to consumers. The last sentence is evaluative, although it could be further developed. d Another effective paragraph considers the possible benefits of good deflation for businesses together with some evaluation. e There is a clear reference to the problems associated with 'bad' deflation to the economy, illustrated with an accurate *AD/AS* diagram. f This paragraph develops the possible reasons why bad deflation might have undesirable consequences for the economy. g It is followed by an effective paragraph which explains the disadvantages of bad deflation to consumers and workers with some evaluation in the last sentence. h There is consideration of the possible problems of bad deflation for businesses together with some evaluation. i This paragraph is evaluative because it focuses on the potential problems associated with deflation. j An effective concluding paragraph synthesises the arguments set out previously, although it does not make reference to the wording of the question, which refers to a 'sustained period of deflation'.

Overall, this is a very sound response which follows a logical progression. The distinction between two causes of deflation is helpful in analysing the benefits and costs of deflation. The points made are evaluated, although in some cases they could be developed more fully. There is, however, an attempt to provide a conclusion.

Question 8 Appreciation of the dollar

Evaluate the economic effects of a significant appreciation in the exchange rate of the US dollar.

(25 marks)

ⓔ As with the previous question, the command word indicates that evaluation must be an essential and significant part of the answer because it is worth 9 marks. The marks for the other assessment objectives are: knowledge 4; application 4; and analysis 8. The focus of the answer may not just be on the USA but also on the USA's trading partners.

Student answer

The growth of globalisation over the last 30 years has led to the increasing interdependence of economies. Since the USA is still the largest player in the global economy, then any change in the value of the dollar is likely to have a considerable impact on the world economy. ⓐ

When the dollar appreciates against other currencies US exports appear relatively more expensive while US imports from abroad appear relatively cheaper. This loss in competitiveness of US goods and services will be detrimental for domestic producers but will benefit foreign producers. However, this will depend on the price elasticity of demand for both US goods and foreign goods: for example, if demand by US citizens for foreign goods is very price elastic then the fall in price of imported goods will cause a more than proportionate rise in demand for imports, so causing a significant loss of revenue for domestic producers. ⓑ

Furthermore, the likely consequence of an increase in imports and decrease in exports is a deterioration in the US current account of the balance of payments. However, this deterioration in the current account will only occur if the Marshall–Lerner condition is fulfilled, i.e. that the sum of the PED for exports and imports is greater than 1. Even then there might be a short-run improvement in the US current account. This would be because contracts have been signed and must be fulfilled, so making demand for imports and exports price inelastic in the short run. However, as new contracts are signed, demand should become more price elastic in the long run, so causing a deterioration in the current account in the long run. ⓒ

Therefore, with the US dollar appreciating, some developing countries will start to find it more burdensome to service their debt. As a result, inequality in the global economy may increase as the poorer countries will face an increased burden of servicing their debt. However, this may be offset by other factors such as increased trade or aid. ⓓ Foreign holders of US treasury bonds would benefit from an appreciation in the value of their holdings. This would have a significant impact on China, which is the world's largest holder of US Treasury bills. ⓔ

The appreciation in the value of the dollar could have an adverse effect on aggregate demand in the USA if it results in an increase in the value of imports and a decrease in the value of imports. This would cause a fall in real output and would lead to an increase in unemployment. In turn, higher unemployment could cause a fall in consumption and in investment, so causing a further fall in aggregate demand. However, the reduced price of imports would decrease inflationary pressures in the USA. On the other hand, the fall in the value of the dollar would increase the competitiveness of goods and services produced in other countries, which could act to boost the economies of these countries, especially those which conduct a significant amount of trade with the USA. f

🄴 **23/25 marks awarded.** a The student begins with an effective introduction which explains the significance of the dollar in the global economy. b This is a relevant point which clearly shows the impact on the global economy. The last sentence of this paragraph contains evaluative comments with the concept of price elasticity of demand applied well. c The possible impact on the US current account is an important area for discussion which lends itself to evaluation, as demonstrated well by the student's response. d This is a good point which is useful in examining the possible impact on developing countries with relevant evaluation. e A further valid point is made which could have significant implications. f The final paragraph explains some effects on aggregate demand with some relevant evaluative points.

Overall, this is a sound answer which includes analysis and evaluation of a variety of issues, although the analysis might be enhanced with an *AD/AS* diagram.

■ Paper 3

Question 9 The Trans-Pacific Partnership (TPP)

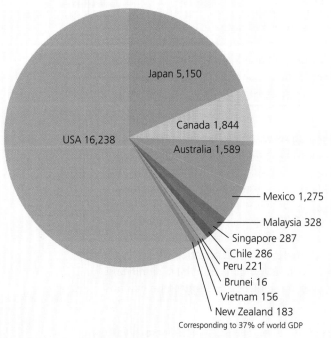

USA 16,238
Japan 5,150
Canada 1,844
Australia 1,589
Mexico 1,275
Malaysia 328
Singapore 287
Chile 286
Peru 221
Brunei 16
Vietnam 156
New Zealand 183
Corresponding to 37% of world GDP

Figure 1 Size of the 12 TPP countries (GDP $bn, 2013)

Economic component	Trillion yen (¥)
Consumption	3.0
Investment	0.5
Exports	2.6
Imports	2.9
NB Agricultural and fishery production is predicted to fall by ¥3.0 trillion	

Figure 2 Estimate of the impact of membership of TPP on the Japanese economy

Extract 1: The Trans-Pacific Partnership (TPP)

It is expected that, during the course of 2015, an enormous new trading bloc, the Trans-Pacific Partnership (TPP), will be formed consisting of 12 countries: the USA, Australia, Brunei Darussalam, Canada, Chile, Japan, Malaysia, Mexico, New Zealand, Peru, Singapore and Vietnam. This trading bloc would represent about 40% of the world's GDP and a third of total world trade.

The primary aim of the TPP is to increase world trade by reducing protectionism in the areas of government contracts for major investment projects, intellectual property and the conduct of state-owned enterprises (SOEs). Currently, it is believed that Chinese SOEs enjoy unfair access to licences, contracts and state finance, giving them an unfair advantage over companies in other countries. However, reducing such protectionism may be difficult. For example, it may not be possible to regulate Vietnamese SOEs, which are allegedly used by senior Communist party officials as a means of generating revenues for favoured projects and sometimes for personal gain. Meanwhile the state-owned Japanese Post Office may not meet rules currently being negotiated.

Those in favour of the TPP argue that it will be the most important contribution to a reduction in trade barriers this century as well as reducing non-tariff barriers. For the USA, it would also help to ensure that it has more influence in Asia and that China does not become too powerful in the region.

However, opponents of the TPP consider that it would become too powerful in the world economy and that its policies would endanger food safety, access to medicines and national sovereignty. For example, the USA is concerned that it would be forced to import from Vietnam seafood that fails to meet existing American safety standards.

Extract 2: The TPP and Japan's agricultural industry

Japanese farmers are among the most protected in the world, with high subsidies and price supports. Indeed, half of average incomes comes from subsidies and price supports, according to the OECD. This compares with one-fifth in the EU and one-tenth in the USA. Japan relies proportionally more on trade barriers to support farmers than other countries do. The USA and the EU began shifting from tariffs to direct subsidies in the 1960s, but in Japan farmers receive more than twice as much income from tariff-based price supports as they do from subsidies. In effect, the government has left much of the burden of supporting farmers to consumers, who pay significantly more for food and particularly for rice than they would without barriers to trade.

Farmers account for less than 4% of Japan's workforce and generate just 1% of its GDP. Nevertheless, support for import barriers by Japan's agriculture ministry and by farmers has made Japan unwilling to sign trade deals which involve a reduction in protectionist measures. The agriculture ministry has said that without trade barriers Japan's agricultural output could decrease by 50%.

Despite all the protection they receive, Japan's rice farmers produce a third less than they did 20 years ago. This is a result of a decline in the rural population and a government policy of reducing the amount of land for rice production in order to maintain high prices. It has been argued that costs could be reduced by 50% with bigger farms, and also that farmers could profit by developing markets targeting high-income consumers abroad. The Japanese Prime Minister and his advisers think freer trade would boost Japan's economy by improving access to foreign markets for manufacturers and forcing protected local industries such as agriculture to become more productive.

(a) With reference to Figure 2, explain the likely effect on Japan's GDP of its membership of the TPP. (5 marks)

e This question demands clear reference to Figure 2 (actual figures should be included in the answer), followed by a written explanation.

(b) With reference to Extract 2, examine what might be inferred about elasticities of demand for imported rice and domestically produced rice in Japan. (8 marks)

e Initially, consideration must be given as to which elasticities of demand are relevant. Then appropriate use must be made of the information provided. Finally, evaluation is required because the command word is 'examine'.

(c) With reference to the last paragraph of Extract 2, assess reasons why a country such as Japan might have trade barriers to protect the agricultural industry. (12 marks)

ⓔ Again, evaluation is required because the command word is 'assess'. It is also important to discuss reasons for protectionism in the context of Japan's agricultural industry.

EITHER

(d) Evaluate the possible microeconomic and macroeconomic effects of an increase in foreign direct investment on Japan's industries and on its economy. (25 marks)

ⓔ It is important to ensure there is both depth of analysis and breadth in the answer. In particular, both microeconomic and macroeconomic effects must be considered. It is also necessary to relate the analysis to the context of the question, i.e. the impact of an increase in FDI on the Japanese economy. Given that 'evaluate' is the command word, the points considered should be evaluated.

OR

(e) Evaluate the likely microeconomic and macroeconomic effects of the removal of tariffs on Japan's agricultural industry. (25 marks)

ⓔ As with (d), it is important to ensure there is both depth of analysis and breadth in the answer. In particular, both microeconomic and macroeconomic effects must be considered. It is also necessary to relate the analysis to the context of the question, i.e. effects of the removal of tariffs on Japan's agricultural industry. Given that 'evaluate' is the command word, the points considered should be evaluated.

> **Student answer**
>
> **(a)** According to the data in Figure 2, Japan's GDP might be expected to rise. Aggregate demand is calculated as follows:
>
> consumption + investment + government expenditure + exports – imports
>
> Therefore,
>
> ¥3.0 trillion + ¥0.5 trillion + ¥2.6 trillion – ¥2.9 trillion = + ¥3.2 trillion
>
> However, this is only an estimate and this may not turn out to be true. Also, the impact on agriculture and fishing may have a larger negative impact on GDP than predicted.

ⓔ 5/5 marks awarded. This is a good approach to answering this question: the elements of aggregate demand have been identified and then the data are used appropriately.

> **(b)** Price elasticity of demand (PED) refers to the responsiveness of quantity demanded to a change in price. **ⓐ** Since rice is a staple food and is eaten regularly by Japanese citizens, it is likely that demand will be price inelastic, i.e. a price change will cause a less than proportionate change in quantity demanded. Therefore, the value of PED will lie between 0 and –1. **ⓑ**

Imported rice and domestically produced rice are likely to be good substitutes. Their relationship may be analysed with reference to cross elasticity of demand. This refers to the responsiveness of quantity demanded for one product to a change in the price of another product. In this case, a fall in the price of imported rice would cause a fall in the demand for domestically produced rice. 🅒

🅮 **7/8 marks awarded.** 🅐 It is good practice to begin with a definition of a term to be employed in the analysis. 🅑 The rest of the paragraph applies the concept of price elasticity effectively and it is well related to the context. 🅒 This paragraph includes an accurate definition of cross elasticity of demand and applies the concept well by explaining that imported rice and domestically produced rice are likely to be good substitutes. The only omission is that it could be stated that the cross elasticity of demand would be positive.

(c) Countries might take measures to protect agriculture because they may want to maintain security of food supplies and not be dependent on imported food. If a country has to import much of its food then this could contribute to a trade deficit. 🅐

Further, farming is a precarious industry: prices tend to fluctuate considerably because both demand and supply are very price inelastic. Consequently, changes in supply or demand would cause prices to change significantly. This would make it difficult for farmers to plan investment and output. 🅑

Some countries defend protectionist measures for agriculture because they wish to preserve and support rural communities and the rural way of life. 🅒

However, protectionism might lead to a misallocation of resources and higher prices for consumers. 🅓

🅮 **9/12 marks awarded.** 🅐 This is a valid reason and includes the use of the concept 'trade deficit'. 🅑 Again, this paragraph considers an important issue and applies economic concepts appropriately. 🅒 The student makes a brief but valid point. 🅓 This is a brief but relevant piece of evaluation.

Overall, this is a good answer but more development is needed, especially in evaluation.

(d) Inward investment by transnational companies (TNCs) is usually regarded positively because of its huge impact on economic growth: inward investment is an injection into the circular flow of income of an economy, causing the aggregate demand curve to shift to the right. 🅐

In the long run the aggregate supply curve will also shift to the right because the investment causes an increase in the country's productive capacity. The following diagram shows an increase in real output from Y_1 to Y_3. 🅑

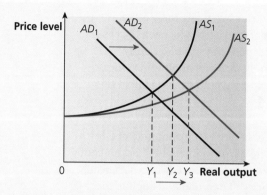

Investment by TNCs usually involves technology transfer — this occurs when the TNC invests in another country and brings in new technology which can significantly increase productivity. In turn, domestic producers may copy this technology and so increase their productivity also. Technology transfer will also help to cause the long-run aggregate supply curve to shift to the right and so cause a fall in the price level.

In the same way, the TNC might introduce new, more efficient managerial and production techniques which may also lead to higher productivity and greater productive efficiency. Both new technology and more efficient management techniques could lead to a reduction in average costs of firms in the industry and so to an increase in their profits. Further, other firms in the industry could benefit if they copy these techniques. Sometimes, FDI by TNCs includes the building of new infrastructure such as roads which could help to reduce transport costs for firms in the area. **c**

TNCs provide employment opportunities for the population and may improve human capital (the skills and expertise of the workforce) by providing training and education programmes to increase workers' skills. This would also increase productivity. However, TNCs may bring highly skilled managers and workers from abroad and only provide opportunities for unskilled workers in the host country or exploit workers by making them work long hours in poor conditions for very low wages. There is also a danger that domestic firms may not be able to compete with the TNC and go out of business, so the net increase in employment may not be great. **d**

A major benefit from the FDI from the TNC might be an improvement in the balance of payments: the initial investment will cause an inflow into the financial account of the balance of payments and, once production is underway, there should be an improvement in the current account when some of the goods produced are exported. However, in the longer term, interest, profits and dividends may be repatriated to the shareholders of the company, which would have a negative impact on the current account. **e**

The government of the country receiving the FDI might benefit from an increase in tax revenues because the TNC would be providing more employment and so there would be more workers paying income tax. Further, these workers may be spending more money and so the government would receive higher tax revenues from expenditure taxes. The TNC itself may be paying corporation tax to the government. However, price transfer techniques may be employed, by which the TNC ensures that it makes most profit in the country where corporation tax is lowest. [f]

Natural resources might be exploited and depleted by the TNC. There is a danger of an increase in external costs associated with the investment. For example, the new factories and infrastructure built by the TNC might have adverse consequences in terms of spoiling of the environment, pollution and waste. However, the government may have more resources to deal with these issues, i.e. from the increase in tax revenues. [g]

ⓔ 22/25 marks awarded. [a] A good point is made but the multiplier concept could be included in the analysis. [b] The diagram is accurate and illustrates clearly the impact of FDI on real output. [c] Both these paragraphs make valid points illustrating the possible benefits of FDI. [d] The potential employment benefit of FDI is often considered to be important: it is analysed and evaluated well in this paragraph. [e] Again, this is an effective paragraph on the implications for the balance of payments, including evaluation. [f] There is a valid argument and evaluation in this paragraph. [g] In essence, this final paragraph is mainly evaluative and contains pertinent concerns about FDI.

Overall, this is a very sound response. However, it could be enhanced by supporting points with specific examples.

(e) Tariffs are taxes on imported goods. If they were removed on food imports then there would be considerable benefits to consumers. For example, the removal of tariffs would result in a fall in prices, which would increase the real incomes of consumers and so increase their living standards. Consumers would also benefit from a greater choice of food products. [a]

The elimination of tariffs will result in lower prices and higher consumer surplus, i.e. the difference between consumers' willingness to pay and the price they actually pay. This is illustrated in the diagram below, which shows that consumer surplus has increased by the area $C + D + E + F$. [b] The welfare gains are triangles D and F.

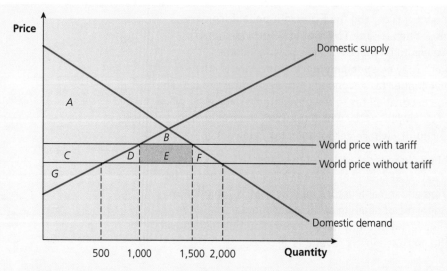

It can be seen that imports will increase from 500 to 1,500 units, increasing choice for consumers in Japan. Further, the imported food will now be more price competitive with domestically produced food. c

However, if the increased foreign competition causes uncompetitive domestic farmers to leave the industry then the increased choice may occur in the short term only. Further, a major foreign supplier may gain a degree of monopoly power and force up prices in the long run. d

If all tariffs are removed then the global economy would benefit from the application of the law of comparative advantage, which states that even if one country has an absolute advantage in the production of all goods, it can still benefit from specialisation and trade if it specialises in the production of goods in which it has a comparative advantage, i.e. in the goods which it can produce at a lower opportunity cost. According to this theory, economic growth would increase and so world living standards would increase. However, the assumptions underlying the law of comparative advantage have been criticised on the grounds that they are unrealistic. For example, it is assumed that costs of production are constant whereas, in practice, diminishing returns are likely to set in at some point, causing a rise in short-run average costs. Further, transport costs are assumed to be zero whereas it is possible that high transport costs could offset any potential gains from comparative advantage. e

The Japanese government will face a loss of tax revenue after the removal of tariffs (area E in the diagram). While this may be relatively insignificant it should be remembered that Japan has been running a fiscal deficit and has a national debt of over 230% of GDP.

The removal of tariffs might act as an incentive for businesses to become more efficient. For example, it states in Extract 2 that 'costs could be reduced by 50% with bigger farms'. In other words it is likely that by mergers and takeovers, larger farmers could benefit from economies of scale (where an increase in the scale of production leads to a more than proportionate increase in output and so to a fall in long-run average costs). For example, technical economies of scale might include the use of sophisticated spraying machines and combine harvesters. However, if the firms grow too large, there is a danger that they will suffer from diseconomies of scale — rising long-run average costs as output increases. The extract also states that 'farmers could profit by...targeting high-income consumers abroad'. This implies that farmers should produce food which has an income elastic demand rather than staple products such as rice. For example, countries such as Chile have diversified agricultural output into exotic fruits such as mangoes and blueberries, which command a high price in many countries. However, there is a danger that in times of recession, there would be a more than proportionate fall in demand for such products. 📖

ⓔ **20/25 marks awarded.** 🄰 The answer starts with a good introduction. 🄱 It is good practice to apply concepts learned in previous themes because Paper 3 is synoptic.

🄲 The diagram is well integrated into the written analysis and is used to illustrate some key points arising from the removal of tariffs. 🄳 This paragraph includes good examples of evaluative comments. 🄴 Here some relevant analysis and evaluation of the theory of comparative advantage could be illustrated by a numerical example. 📖 This is a good paragraph which focuses on microeconomic effects, applying appropriate concepts, and includes evaluative comments.

Overall, this is a sound response covering a variety of effects. It could, perhaps include a concluding paragraph.

Knowledge check answers

1 It could limit globalisation if higher transport costs make it less likely for firms to relocate production plants or service activities abroad.

2 Those countries with very low savings ratios are more likely to have current account deficits on the balance of payments because a low savings ratio implies a high propensity to consume, with an associated high level of imports.

3 Free trade enables countries to specialise according to the law of comparative advantage, which will lead to increased output and, therefore, to higher living standards. For consumers, there should be more choice and lower prices, and firms should benefit from larger markets and economies of scale.

4 An increase in export prices; a decrease in import prices; an appreciation in the exchange rate of a country's currency.

5 Free trade between member countries.

6 The size of the tariff, as well as the price elasticity of demand and the domestic price elasticity of supply. If demand and supply are both price elastic, the tariff will be more effective in reducing imports.

7 Various factors could be responsible, including: relatively low unit labour costs; relatively high productivity; a relatively low inflation rate; undervaluation of the currency; non-price-competitive advantages such as design, quality and reliability of the product.

8 Expenditure-switching policies relate to policies designed to change the composition of expenditure between domestic and foreign goods, e.g. tariffs, whereas expenditure-reducing policies are designed to reduce aggregate demand, e.g. contractionary fiscal policy.

9 This could result in a loss of confidence in the currency, so causing its value to fall. However, if defaulting countries left the eurozone, leaving just the strong members, then the euro would probably rise in value.

10 The current account would deteriorate, i.e. the deficit would get larger, since the Marshall–Lerner condition had not been fulfilled.

11 That country's international competitiveness would decline, since a relatively lower productivity rate implies that its unit costs of production would rise relative to its competitors.

12 No: a fall in absolute poverty may be caused by rising real incomes but relative poverty could actually increase because the latter measures the proportion of people below a set level, e.g. 60% of the median income.

13 The Lorenz curve would move further away from the 45° line.

14 Many hard commodities such as cotton and iron ore are raw materials used to manufacture goods required for everyday purposes, while soft commodities such as wheat and rice are part of the staple diets of many people Therefore, the demand for both hard and soft commodities tends to rise proportionately less than increases in real income.

15 The marginal propensity to save is likely to be low because poor people have to spend a high proportion of their incomes simply to provide for their basic human needs.

16 It will increase because there will be more dependants, i.e. those under 16 and over 65, relative to the number of workers.

17 If individuals have no property rights, they will not have any collateral to secure a loan from a bank to start a business.

18 Producers in developed countries may have monopsony power, enabling them to drive down the prices they pay for goods from producers in developing countries.

19 Market-orientated strategies include trade liberalisation and removal of government subsidies. Interventionist strategies include managed exchange rates and development of human capital.

20 Kenya and Mexico.

21 FDI is undertaken by transnational companies with the aim of making a profit for shareholders, whereas aid refers to grants or loans at less than the market rate of interest (called concessional loans) given to developing countries by governments, international organisations or non-government organisations.

22 This refers to the interest paid on loans. In the case of a government, it means that it would have less money available to spend on public services.

23 There is a danger that countries whose debts have been cancelled will follow policies that result in further debts being built up in the future.

24 It has loaned money to countries such as Greece, Ireland and Portugal in an attempt to prevent their governments defaulting on their debts. Strict conditions are attached to these loans, e.g. austerity measures to reduce fiscal deficits.

25 A bank failure could cause problems for consumers and businesses that are not customers of the bank. For example, firms (which do not have accounts at the bank) may face a loss of trade because customers of the bank may have lost all their deposits.

26 Non-excludability, i.e. it is impossible to prevent people from consuming a product once it is provided; and non-rivalry, i.e. consumption by one person does not limit consumption by others.

27 When income tax rises, people will substitute away from work to leisure because the opportunity cost of work is now lower, i.e. the loss of earnings from work is now lower. (This is called the substitution effect.)

28 It would cause the value of the multiplier to fall because leakages would have risen.

29 It is likely that public finances would deteriorate: automatic stabilisers mean that government expenditure on social benefits for the unemployed would increase, while tax revenues would fall (not only from incomes but also from a reduction in revenues from expenditure taxes, e.g. VAT, and from corporation tax).

30 Banks might be charging considerably higher interest rates on loans than the Bank of England's base rate. Further, banks may be unwilling to lend if they consider the risks of non-repayment to be too great. A lack of confidence might mean that firms and consumers are unwilling to borrow.

Index

Note: Page numbers in **bold** indicate key term definitions.

Index